RICHARD BEN CRAMER

Bob Dole

Richard Ben Cramer is the author of *What
It Takes*. He is a recipient of the Pulitzer
Prize for his work for the *Philadelphia In-
quirer*. He lives with his wife and daughter
in Maryland.

Also by RICHARD BEN CRAMER

What It Takes

Bob Dole

Bob Dole

BY RICHARD BEN CRAMER

VINTAGE BOOKS

A Division of Random House, Inc.

New York

FIRST VINTAGE BOOKS EDITION, SEPTEMBER 1995

Copyright © 1992, 1995 by Richard Ben Cramer

Library of Congress Cataloging-in-Publication Data
Cramer, Richard Ben.
Bob Dole / Richard Ben Cramer.
p.   cm.
ISBN 0-679-76647-2
1. Dole, Robert J., 1923–   . 2. Legislators—United States—
Biography.   3. United States. Congress. Senate—Biography.
I. Title.
E840.8.D64C73   1995
973.927092—dc20
[B]   95-17436
CIP

Author photograph © Sarah Leen

Manufactured in the United States of America

10   9   8   7   6   5   4   3   2   1

Contents

Author's Note

There's that famous old saw about American lives—they have no second acts. Bob Dole has already disproved that. But I always thought it was true, at least, about American books. Now we'll put that to the test.

What It Takes, the story of six men who bent their lives to the hugely public gamble of running for President, came out in '92. In a thousand pages it showed, I hope, that campaigns for President aren't about the sound bites, thirty-second ad spots, and poll results that pass as news in our elections. A candidacy is the sum of a long life's doing . . . and the poor stunned soul whom we finally shove into the Oval Office has only his own life's methods with which to confront the job.

So now, as another election approaches, I thought it worthwhile to pull from those pages the life story of Bob Dole. It's a story that spans most of our century, starting in Depression dust bowl Kansas . . . and though it informs his every political act, it always seemed to me much larger than his politics. Dole is one man who has endured, suffered, and triumphed through the greatest events of our time.

There's another old saw by which I will abide—you can't change history. In these pages, I see infelicities I could rewrite, certainties of which I'm now less certain, and hints I could write now as facts. But *What It Takes* is part of my history, too. I resisted the urge to rewrite it all to reflect the (supposed) verities of 1995. Instead, I went back this spring to visit with Dole, and I have added a new introduction, to give this small book a present tense.

I am grateful to Senator Dole for that visit, and for the patient kindness with which he has always treated me. I am grateful also to Marty Asher of Vintage Books, who gave my work a second act. And I thank Carolyn White, my wife and my number-one editor, who put this book together with her lovely care and skill.

Richard Ben Cramer
Chestertown, Maryland
April 1995

Introduction

I see him again—first time in three years—steaming through the double doors of a big Florida hotel ballroom, straight up the aisle, past five hundred prosperous pink men, making for the head table and his speech. From across the room, he looks the same: still, there's not a wrinkle in his dark Brooks Brothers suit; his silk tie is knotted tight against the smooth collar of his white shirt; his hair is dark, softly in place (four strokes with the barber comb, still in his back pants pocket); his face is still handsome, tight with perpetual tan. (It's like even his skin is practiced: Dole can get a tan on the way from his car to the hotel door.)

There is the same purposeful speed to his walk, as he blows past the pink men, to the front of the room. These are the Big Guys of the textile industry—$137 billion in annual sales, CEOs and COOs—and some of them know Dole. That's why he's moving fast, to get by before anyone can ask him for anything. That's why his wave (to one Big Guy who has caught his eye) is a quick left palm with the fingers upraised—at full reach, not even wiggling . . . on a football field, it's called a stiffarm.

He has his other arm bent at his midriff, as he always carries it before him in the world. Most people in that room know the right arm is useless, almost paralyzed, but even those who've known him for years think all the operations must have cocked the arm in front of him, fused the bones so the arm bends from the elbow to look almost like a working arm. In fact, it's Dole who makes it look like a working arm. If he ever let himself rest, that arm would hang straight down, visibly shorter than his left arm, with the palm of his right hand twisted toward the back. But Dole never lets anybody see that—his "problem." He keeps a plastic pen in his crooked right fist to round its shape. If he ever let that pen go, the hand would splay, with the forefinger pointing and the others cramped in toward the palm, the back of the hand painfully hollow where doctors, long ago, failed to graft in tendons. But no one ever sees that, either: no matter how many hours he's been up, no matter how long he stays out, no matter how that fist aches or spasms, Dole holds on—against his problem.

He's been doing it so long, you can't even see the moves— he's magician-quick. Now, on the dais, as one of the CEOs raises his right arm to clap ol' Bob on the back, Dole moves *instantly*: a quarter-turn toward the man, and just a foot backward, with his camera-perfect grin of delight—like he, just that very second, had in mind to turn and greet that Big Guy—with his left hand swinging up to waist level . . . so the CEO's arm drops in midslap, and his palm settles warmly into the Senator's good hand. Dole can't have his reconstructed back and shoulder knocked around by eager boyos.

With Dole it's so quick, you can't call it forethought. After so many years, you can't call it instinct. It's always practiced, and always made new—as it is with the greatest athletes, like Michael Jordan, on his way to the hoop for the millionth time . . . and for the millionth time, making it up as the instant dictates. It's like a dance: he feels the music, and he *can't slow down* . . . no one slows down Bob Dole. They put him on to speak the minute he hits the room.

"A man of character, and integrity . . ."

This is Lauch Faircloth, a first-term Senator from North Carolina. He's in Florida to suck up to the textile kings—and to Dole. He's already winding up his introduction.

". . . Bob Dole leads like a President.

"He looks like a President.

"He acts like a President . . .

"And he's gonna BE President. . . ."

This is the music that Dole likes best.

———

"Thank you . . . I, uh . . ."

Dole pretends to look at his notes while they keep clapping. Half of them are standing to applaud before he's even said a word.

"Well, thank you very much. I'm glad to be here, today . . ."

You can hear him perfectly over the noise. Dole's hard-voweled rasp was made for the distance and mean wind of the prairie. And the voice, like the rest of him, hasn't changed. It's like some devil-deal, like there's some secret portrait of Dole, that's getting old, weak, and ugly in his attic at home . . . except there's no attic in his Watergate apartment. Just a bedroom and a half, a living room, a kitchenette . . . still the bachelor pad he got twenty years ago, after his divorce. When he remarried in

'76, Elizabeth just moved in. Bob never could see the point of a bigger place. He's not home much. What would he do there?

". . . Course, Senators like to talk. Y'may have seen the budget debate—my friend on the Democratic side, Bob Byrd— he talks about *Roman History* . . ."

The fact is, Dole is at home right now—Saturday morning, 10:00 A.M., a thousand miles under his belt this weekend . . . to another hotel, another podium, another crowd of Important Suits . . . and he's relaxing.

"Little bitta Balanced Budget Amendment.

"Little more Roman Hist'ry. . . .

"I even contacted *C-Span*—see if we could get *college credit* . . .

"But I am very glad to be here today. Because, in my view, the 'Merican Textile Industry . . ."

You can't exactly call it a speech. It's just a bracing stroll through the mind of Bob Dole—so much going on! It's mostly Senate stuff—the line-item veto, budget cuts, Medicaid, a joke about Strom Thurmond . . . it drives his handlers nuts. They keep telling him, "Senator, stay on the message!" It drives his hyperdisciplined wife nuts. She rehearses every speech. Bob just gets up and *talks*.

"Well, I'm sorry 'Lizabeth couldn't be here," Dole says to the textile Bigs. He always mentions his powerful wife. She's a major campaign asset. "She had to go to Indiana. She's President of the Red Cross, you know . . ."

Dole has the timing of a professional comic.

"She got to be President. More'n I can say for me . . ."

As always, the laughter in the hall is a low, appreciative, knowing male chuckle. Now, he's rolling.

"But I usually don't bring her to these big meetings . . . she always wants to start a blood drive.

"Kinda messy . . ."

Dole waits for the laughter to subside.

"You may not know this . . .

"But I *ran* for President . . ."

Dole has been making jokes about his campaigns for fifteen years. Actually, it's almost two full decades, if you count (as Dole does) from the day in 1976 when he lost the Vice Presidency on the ticket with Gerald Ford.

In 1980, he stepped into the ring on his own, and flew around the country for a year, promising to whip inflation, wipe out the deficit, and fix the economy . . . but he couldn't even fix his own campaign. He had no organization—he ran everything himself, from his plane. And when he got to the first primary, New Hampshire, he got . . . six hundred votes. It was a total humiliation. What could he do but turn it into a joke?

In '88, he said he'd learned his lesson: he started early, he raised a ton of money, he hired on Big Guys to *organize* the Dole campaign. And it worked—for a while. Dole organized Iowa down to the corncobs, he won the caucus . . . and by the time he steamed into New Hampshire, he was the front-runner—eight points up on the panicky George Bush. But Bush launched a frenzy of campaigning, and filled the state's airwaves with slashing attack ads . . . while Dole and his Big Guys sat on their hands. In six days, their lead was gone. Bush was on his way to the White House. Dole went back to making jokes.

"I remember, in the hotel, three days before New Hampshire, my pollster was whistling 'Hail to the Chief' . . .

"I looked around. I was the only other guy in the room . . .

"Haven't seen that pollster since.

"Haven't paid him either, come to think of it.

"But I do wanta just say one word about the, uh, *next* election. . . . Because I know somebody who's running in 1996."

———

With Dole, it's always the next election, the next, and the next. Even now, in his eighth decade on the planet, after thirty-five years in Congress, and twenty years running for national office, he says—as he always has said: it's different, this time, he's better.

This time, a lot of people think he's right—they're writing about the New Bob Dole—they say he seems comfier. (And, look! His early polls are great!)

But what is the difference?

It's not new issues—though, each time, he has some new wrinkle. Now, he's into the heart of his message, and he pulls from his pocket the Tenth Amendment to the Constitution. It's about reserving power to the States and to the people. This is the new Dole-code for cutting out federal programs: send the power back to the states, and stop piling up debt in Washington. He calls this "reining in government."

Then he turns to foreign policy, and he talks about protecting American interests—with or without resolutions from the UN, with or without any help from our allies. That's the new Dole-code for America First. He calls this "reasserting our place in the world."

But Dole has been talking about budget cuts ever since he got to Washington and had his first meeting with the President—Ike. Even when it wasn't popular (when Ronald Reagan sat in Ike's old chair, and deficits weren't supposed to matter),

Dole still made the budget and debt his overriding issues. No matter how much he wanted the votes of right-wing, supply-side Republicans . . . no matter how many consultants told him to make his message more upbeat . . . no one could ever convince Dole that deficits would simply "grow away." Bobby Joe Dole grew up in Russell, Kansas. He saw people die from debt.

And Dole never talked about a "Global Community," a Post–Cold War World Order, or any of the other buzzwords invented to mask our confusion, once the Soviet Wicked Witch melted away. In Dole's view, the world will always call on American boys to fight and die, somewhere, in troubles not of their own making. Lieutenant R. Dole learned that the hard way, fifty years ago. He feels that, still, every day. It changed his life.

In the end, that's what Dole brings to the table—in this election, every election—his life: only the code words change.

Maybe it is different, this time. Maybe Dole's soaring polls won't melt in the sun . . . because that life looks better to us. Maybe we're on the rebound, after our fling with the overfed uncertainties of the Baby Boom . . . and we value the verities of a man old enough to have had *no choice.* Maybe we'll decorate our century's end with an emblem of the hard past, honestly scarred . . . like we grace our fashion ads or fancy store windows with a beat-up old leather suitcase.

He's telling the Textiles, at the close, about his announcement tour and its big finish in Russell, Kansas—April 14, 1995—fifty years to the day since German steel wrecked his young body. Then he tells them about a trip last year, to the beaches of Normandy, fifty years after D-Day. "I was coming back, after that trip. And, I guess, in the final analysis, I decided maybe there was one more chance, one more opportunity for service—for my generation—one more mission . . ."

And now, all the Textiles stand to cheer. They're still clapping after Dole has shaken hands with all the Bigs on stage and, with purposeful speed, left the ballroom.

———————

Of course, every candidate for President thinks he has What It Takes. These are men (these days—still—they are all men) of personal power: people change their lives for them. They are men of will, ambition, faith. They are men with a lifelong habit of winning. But no one gets through this on habit.

No one can rise at dawn, in another unlovely motel room, to stand outside in bone-aching cold, shaking hands at some factory gate ("How y'doin?" "Hi!" "G'mornin' . . .") for an hour, before his breakfast speech at the coffee shop ("I'm here to tell you, this morning, YOU can make that difference!"), before he piles into a rent-a-car for a half-hour ride to a high school assembly (". . . Because that future is up to YOU . . ."), then forty-five minutes to his coffee-klatsch in the next county ("And I especially want to thank our hostess . . ."), and his luncheon speech over chicken-and-mashed at the motel two counties after that ("I'm here to tell you, today, that YOU . . ."), and his meeting with the local editorial board ("Senator, shouldn't timber products be exempted from the Uruguay Round?"), before his long car ride in the rent-a-car backseat with a feature writer from Chicago ("Did you feel you could never really please your father?"), while he's lurching through traffic in the major market for *Live at Five* with the local anchors ("Senator, thanks for being with us! Why do think you're losing in the polls?"), before his cocktail remarks to fifty big givers ("I'm here to tell you, tonight, that YOU . . ."), and his town meeting at the community center ("I'm glad you asked that, because, as you know, Social Security . . ."), until his body man finally pulls him out, and he's driven through the night to an airport motel, where he's handed eight call slips that ought to be returned—fast, so he can get his sleep. If he gets everybody on the phone, straight-away, he'll have five or six hours till wheels up and an hour's flight, to another state, to do it again . . .

No one can do that day after day, week after week, *for years* . . . without some rock-hard certainty that can't be milled away by nonsense and stress. He has to know: Why him? And: Why now? . . . He has to know that he is The One.

And if he's strong enough to keep going—if he's able, smart, and lucky—then, he'll get to the final twist in the road, when things catch fire, he can see how his words make the people feel, he can feel how those words now matter *to him*. He can make all the difference just by walking into a room. There are thousands of people—and they want *him*. He and his campaign fill the lives of people who are almost strangers, and he takes over the life of everyone dear to him. He has to, it's all right—because *it's that important*. Now, he knows:

Not only should I be President, *I am going to be President!*

At that point, his idea of himself will change—has to change—so he can see in himself a figure of size to bestride a chunk of history. He will make war and peace, guide the nation, and change 250 million lives . . . an age of those lives will bear his name forever . . . his name and his face, his wife, kids, and dog, will be known to billions—across the planet—they'll look to him, listen to him, depend on him . . . he will bend the story of mankind on earth.

And after that, alas, by the nature of the process, all but one man will lose.

This is loss that's almost impossible to deal with. It's horribly public—a great national fireball of failure, in a country that reviles its losers. But that's not the worst part: it's the loss inside that won't let you rest. These habitual winners have bent the world to their will for their whole lives—forever. If they could see it in their minds, they could make it happen . . . and now, for the first time, they have to come to terms with how they saw so wrongly. This is loss that makes you question your life. But there's more—and worse: for now that life has changed. Or it's gone. It just doesn't fit anymore . . . once you've seen yourself so differently . . . and huge . . . you can't go back. Win or lose, your life, as you knew it, is over.

That's What It Takes. It takes your life.

It takes your life away, and replaces it for a while with a strange, intoxicating hyperexistence—awesome and full of import . . . and when that's over, if you lose that, then you don't know anything about yourself—save that nothing will feel quite like life again, except another dose of the same.

And if you've lost it for good, if you know you can't make it happen again, then it feels like there's nothing at all—like a death.

Bob Dole has been there.

It was in '88, after that fateful week in New Hampshire. Dole thought that was his time—he was winning! At last! It was going to be him! . . . But Bush campaigned as he never had before—flung himself all over the state—truck stops, McDonald's, 7-Elevens, *parking lots* . . . and George Bush stole Dole's dream away.

It was that night, after the vote. Dole couldn't sleep at all. It all kept replaying in his head. All the work—all the people who helped him, and never took a dime, never asked for anything—they just wanted . . . *him.*

He blamed himself—what was *wrong* with him? He thought of a hundred things he could've done—could have *tried*. God knows, he tried, but . . .

He lay there all night, tried to lie still . . . until he couldn't try anymore, and it was five o'clock and there was no reason to lie in bed. That's when Dole came down to the lobby of his hotel, and sat—no one around, he just sat. Pen in his hand. Careful suit. Perfect shirt, tie. And no one around. What would he have said, anyway? He was sorry? Sorry was the only thing in him.

He knew loss—God knows, he could handle . . . why couldn't he handle *this*? . . . why couldn't he stop his head? Things that could've been different—all the things he'd done . . . probably wrong—half the things . . .

But the worst part wasn't things he'd done. It was the pictures of Bush—that was what he couldn't stop—*pictures of Bush!* In his head! Bush throwing snowballs, driving trucks, forklifts . . . unwrapping his Big Mac. Dole never wanted to see that in his head. And he never wanted to say, even in his head . . .

It would not leave him alone . . . five in the morning! Had to come down to the lobby . . . but he couldn't get away from it. For the first time in his career—first time in thirty years—Bob Dole said to himself:

"Maybe I could have done that . . . if I was whole."

———————

From the seat next to Dole, in the plane back to Washington, now I can see, there's more silver in his hair. There're a few new lines in his face, around his mouth, where skin has sagged. Or maybe it's just the way Dole goes loose when he finally gets to a plane, one of the corporate jets that always seem to be waiting for him. This one's a Lear, and it welcomes Dole's back with soft leather. The body man, Mike Glassner, sits opposite, facing backward, toward Dole. The copilot digs from a bin two small Saran-wrapped platters—sandwiches and fruit—Diet Cokes are in the fridge . . . the door swings shut, the engines rumble . . . and for an hour or two, there will be quiet, nothing pending, and no one who can get to Bob Dole.

"Yeah, I said to 'Lizabeth, if we retire, I think I'll buy a plane.

" 'What for?'

"Agh, I don' know. Jus' to sit in it. Fly around.

"Hegh hegh hegh . . ."

Dole's laughing at his joke. That's how you know it's not a joke. He must have seen my surprise at the word—*retire.*

"I thought about it. Sure. After last time. Couldn't sleep right. Thought about it for a long time. Going over it. For months."

Dole is silent for a moment.

"Thought maybe . . . Got a pretty good life. Home with 'Lizabeth. Sundays, at least. Get out to dinner, every once in a while. Pretty good married life."

But Bush lost, in '92, and that changed everything. People said it was the end of an era—and the end of Republicans in the White House. It was the coming of a new generation—and government as the spearhead of change. It's hard to even remember now how everyone-in-the-know in Washington *knew* the Republicans were clueless—*nowhere*—when Clinton rode in for his honeymoon.

And Dole? Well, he was the Republican Party. Had to be.

The last Big Guy standing. He didn't see any choice. He did what Bob Dole does. He ran with the ball.

"Good news is, Clinton's on his honeymoon," Dole said at the time.

"Bad news is, his chaperone is Bob Dole."

Of course, he took heat for that. Dole remembers it well:

"Yeah, everybody—you're too tough.

"You're too mean.

"You're too this . . . you're too that."

But Dole was right. Clinton started his new age with Gays in the Army. Then he proposed his Stimulus Package—an old-fashioned plate of pork. Dole rallied his troops in the Senate . . . and killed it. Clinton's honeymoon was over. The Republicans were coming back. And they never stopped coming.

"If he'da started off with something else, we'da been quiet as mice . . . didn't happen."

Dole started flyin' around again—this time for the midterm elections. He hit eighty-five House districts himself—five hundred events, forty-seven states . . .

And it was different, better. It wasn't just the Republican tide—though he could feel that: called it, state by state, like Nixon used to do. But something else was different. They wanted . . . him.

Dole's thoughts turn, as always, to New Hampshire.

"Yeah. In '88 we had, by the end—what was it?—seventy-seven hundred volunteers up there. Now we got twenty-three thousand . . .

"Got four outta five on the Governor's Council. Nine outta ten of the Sheriffs—they make a difference."

Nine out of ten?

"One's a Democrat. But we're try'na get him. *Hegh hegh hegh.*"

This time, Dole has the Governors. They're the ones who put Bush over the top.

"Yeah, lot of 'em. Pataki in New York. Voinovich came out early in Ohio—and Speaker of the House there, leader in the Senate . . ."

This time, Dole has a hundred Congressmen.

"House guys, I go to their fund-raisers in Washington. I can hit five a night. Two or three at the Capitol Hill Club, one with the Truckers', one somewhere else . . ."

Dole glances out the window at the sunset. There's a funder in Washington he could stop by, tonight.

"They ask you, you know—they're so pleased, if you actually show up."

"We had a funder in Washington," Glassner, the body man, offers.

"Yeah," Dole says. "Three hundred fifty thousand."

"Right," Glassner says. "But no PACs. Personal checks. Guys in Washington don't write personal checks."

Dole cuts him off with a gesture of his left hand toward his glass of ice. Glassner jumps for the Diet Coke. The pilot's already on the intercom with the weather for D.C.

"Just a half," Dole says—a little glass of caffeine. Probably will stop by that funder, since it's early.

Dole takes a swig, and settles back in companionable silence.

"*Yut dut dut dah . . . dut dut dut dut dah . . .*"

He's tuned in now to the little march that plays in his head. No one knows what song it is—or whether it's a song at all—it's just a syncopated bit of prairie breeze that leaks out of him, when he's happy. I can see what all the writers mean, with that New Dole stuff. "Comfy" is putting it mildly.

I'm watching his profile . . . it's more than comfy. He's free. More than any man in the country, Dole knows What It Takes—a whole life. And he's already given his.

"Uh, Senator? . . ."

I have a question—kind of dumb—but a President question.

". . . If you do get in, what's the first thing? I mean, not the first hundred days, or any of that. But what's the first thing you want to do?"

Dole stops marching, and there's silence. It's the kind of question that every first-timer learns as boilerplate, by the time he's been running for a week.

"Haven't thought . . . ," Dole says. He looks out the window again—dark outside, now. His voice is soft. "If I get elected, at my age, you know . . . I'm not goin' anywhere. It's not an agenda. I'm just gonna serve my country."

There's a lurch as the Lear slows down, over the Potomac. Dole straightens, hands away his glass, and squares himself. He's been doing this so long, he can feel the runway coming. It's going to be a good landing, this time. He knows.

The Lear's door swings open to reveal his Lincoln Town Car, idling on the tarmac in the darkness. I'm trying to thank him for the time, and the ride.

"Agh, gotta gooo!" Dole says. It's the chain-saw voice. He's back to business. Don't slow him down. He makes for the car, and he's gone in twenty seconds. Saturday night. He's got work to do.

Bob Dole

Russell, Kansas

Even back in Russell, Bob Dole had work to do. With Bina Dole driving the train in that house, there were plenty of jobs for the kids. Sometimes, even before school, in the first gray light of day, Bob would run a couple of blocks to Dean Krug's place, on the west edge of town, where the houses stopped and the endless flat fields began. Dean's dad was a carpenter, but he kept cows on the side. At dawn the boys would do the milking, and Mr. Stoppel, at the grocery, would sell the milk at a nickel a quart. If they got five quarts, and Mr. Stoppel sold them all, the money from the fifth went to the boys. If they split the work, they each got two and a half cents.

In the summer, they could get another nickel digging dandelions. Bob and his brother, Kenny, one year younger—and sometimes Dean—would dig weeds from a lawn: five cents a bushel. But they had to pack the basket. If they dug for Bina Dole, she wanted to see the roots.

Then, too, Bob and Kenny sold a patent remedy, the good-for-what-ails-you Cloverine Salve, twenty-five cents a tin. The

3

boys would pay for ten to a shipment, and the goo arrived twelve tins to a pack, so if they sold a whole sleeve—might take weeks —they made fifty cents. Their relatives had enough Cloverine to grease a herd of cows.

Weekends, if there was time, they'd deliver grocery hand-bills. Bob got the job from Mr. Holzer. That was the way it went: Bob got the job; Kenny and Dean would help. They'd get two dollars for the whole town, about eight hundred houses. They'd start on a Friday after school and finish Saturday morning. They couldn't put the flyer in the mailbox because there was no stamp, and that was against postal law. But they couldn't throw it on the lawn, either: old man Holzer would have a fit. So they knocked on every door. And if people weren't home, they could put it in the screen door. It could take an hour to do a square block, but heck, there were whole *families* didn't have two dollars, cash.

Cash was always short in Russell: cash and water—they went hand in hand. Just a few years before the town was founded, as a way station for the Kansas Pacific, most atlases called these plains the Great American Desert. By 1870, the railroad made it through, all the way to Denver, and tried to lure settlers along the way. But Wall Street was convinced there wasn't enough rain on the empty grassland to support agriculture, or a loan for it. Still, railroad agents patrolled the eastern ports, looking for immigrants to break the prairie sod. In the 1870s, the Union Pacific sent scouts to Europe, offering a package deal: steerage across the Atlantic and a boxcar ride to Kansas, for eighty dollars a head.

That's how the land around Russell was settled, with the arrival of the Volga Germans. They were farmers whom Catherine the Great had lured to Russia a hundred years before with a grant of black Volga steppe, and exemption from service in the Russian army for ninety-nine years. Now, in the 1870s, the grant and exemption were running out, and the Volga Germans dispatched scouts to America to find a new land for an old people. They were wheat growers, a hard-headed, tight-fisted bunch. They'd have to be. The railroad never told them about the summers when it never got around to raining; about the plagues of grasshoppers; about the winter storms that screamed in across the plain, swirling snow that could bury a house in its drifts. But the Germans stuck it out, and stuck to their ways. (Sixty years later, in his cream and egg station, Doran Dole, Bob's dad, would use a few words of *Deutsch* to settle accounts on the big cans of milk brought into town by the Volga Germans.)

The Doles had lived through another generation or two in America, on farms in New York and Ohio, before they joined the tide of settlers seeking a fresh start on fresh land, after the Civil War. But Doran's family was one of many in Kansas that came up short in the struggle with the banks, and ended up tenants instead of landowners. They paid a third of their crop to the landlord, and lived on the rest; there wasn't much left. Doran came into Russell for high school, but America was shouldering her burden in the Great War, and Doran dropped out of school to enlist. He wasn't loud about it—Doran wasn't one for speeches about anything—but a call to the flag was, for him, just as basic as the other ineluctables of life: weather, work, and the shortage of cash. When he came back to Russell, he used his Army pay to rent a storefront on Main Street, which he opened as a café, the White Front, in 1920. When he married Bina Talbott, the following year, their honeymoon was a supper, cooked by a couple of friends, and served at one of the two white tables that occupied one side of the White Front Café. That was about all Doran and Bina ever got out of that restaurant. There just weren't enough folks around Russell, Kansas, who had cash to buy a meal on Main Street. By the time their first son, Bob, was born, in 1923, the White Front was a memory, a picture in their album: Doran Dole, scrubbed and proud, his sturdy form wrapped in a long white apron, standing in front of those two white tables and a sign, WE WELCOME YOU, which hung under four small American flags.

After the café closed, Doran opened up the cream and egg station. He bought from the farmers, who'd drop off their milk on their way into town, and he sold to the dairy or the grocery stores. He made about fifteen dollars a week and maybe a dozen eggs, or a quart of cream he'd take home to make butter. Doran was up by 6:00, and in the station by 6:30, getting ready. It had to be just so. He stayed late on Saturday, the farmers' big day in town, and he'd be there after midnight, scrubbing the concrete floor till it shone. If he couldn't bear to work so late, he'd go back Sunday morning, to make sure the place got cleaned just right. He was a strong man, though you wouldn't have noticed, the way he carried himself, so quiet. But a full milk can was near a hundred pounds, and Doran took them to the dock two at a time. He missed one day of work in forty years: spoiled his record, he used to say. But he gladly closed the station every Armistice Day, when the Legion marched up the brick Main Street. And, every year, when they read out the Gettysburg Address, Doran was there in his uniform, sometimes in the color guard. Then, there'd be potluck at Bina's house. That was a big day, Armistice Day.

Fourth of July was special, too, with a feast of Bina's fried chicken and potato salad. There'd be soda pop and watermelon for the kids, before the fireworks. And then the homemade chocolate ice cream. Doran would go to the icehouse and bring back a big block on the morning of the Fourth. Then he'd crush the ice in a gunny sack, and do all the cranking, for hours, by himself. That was before they got the electric icebox. That was a day of miracle! Doran built an extra ledge on the back porch, to hold the thing, and all the Dole kids sat outside, staring . . . waiting. . . . Ice, anytime! Square cubes!

By that time, Doran was managing the elevator for Norris Grain. The money wasn't much more, maybe steadier. The hours were as long, maybe longer. He opened up at 7:00 A.M., with his forty-cup coffee urn already perked. Doran made the strongest coffee in the county—used to fill up the inner basket with grounds level to the rim. He liked it so you could float a spoon, and he liked it hot—a nice, full cup, too. He'd have his gone before yours'd be cool enough to sip. When he'd go to his sisters' houses, they'd worry about making the coffee. If they made him a cup of their regular brew, he'd drink it and say, "Now, how 'bout some coffee?" In the grain elevator, he'd drink it all day, and pass it out to the farmers. He kept chairs and some four-legged stools around, just to make them feel welcome, and they'd all come in on their way out of town. They'd sit in the back, where the earthy grain smell was spiced with the steam from Doran's urn, maybe four or five old German dirt farmers and Doran, all in bib overalls, complaining about the weather, or rust got into the wheat, or something. Every once in a while, Doran would stick in a quiet comment, sometimes advice, more often a joke. He'd tell a newcomer to pull up a stool: "Sure, sit down. Doesn't matter if you work. The gov'ment'll keep you." He'd tell 'em they'd better get back home to collect their "Fare Well" checks. That's what he always called welfare.

He had a way of delivering his lines so you couldn't tell if he was joking. He'd be staring off, at the floor or his single shelf of pesticides, still deadpan, while everybody else in the place cracked up. The farmers called him Doley. He called all the men and boys by name. The girls he called Sis. Mostly, he was just always there, rain or shine, any season, every day. Doran stayed open Thanksgiving if the fall was wet and the milo was late. If the farmers were cutting, he was there. During harvest, when the trucks lined up on Main Street all the way to the highway, he'd work till two in the morning, helping the farmers unload. Then he'd drag himself home for a few hours' sleep, and go at it again the next day. Bina hated that time of year. During harvests, the Dole boys used to run home from school and gulp their lunch, so they could run to the elevator and work for a half-hour while Doran marched home and ate.

During harvests, Bob Dole used to fill a tray with Cokes from the Dawson fountain and pass them out to the farmers sweating in their trucks on Main Street, "Compliments of Dawson Drug . . ." He got the job at the drugstore when he was barely in high school, not yet full-grown. There wasn't any question in the Dawson brothers' minds that he'd do the work, do it seriously. Bobby Dole had always been working, always been serious. The neighbors used to see Bob leave for school in the mornings, as they left for work, walking up Maple Street. He'd run out the door with a whoop— "Bye!"—and off he'd go. Kenny'd come trudging behind. Bob didn't visit with anyone along the way. He seemed to be concentrating. He didn't talk to Kenny, even if Kenny managed to keep up that day. "That Bob! . . . Such a little man!" the neighbor ladies used to tell Bina, who took it as the compliment they probably intended.

There were years at a time when Kenny couldn't keep up,

after he got the infection in his leg. In those days, there were no antibiotics. In Russell, there wasn't even a hospital. The local doctors tried what they knew: they dipped bread in hot milk and stuck a bag of it onto Kenny's leg as a poultice, trying to draw out the disease. They tried to lance the swelling, as they would a boil, but the wounds never healed. There was a doctor named Mead who cut the leg open, swabbed it and drained it, and this time it healed. But Dr. Mead hadn't got it all, and the leg swelled and broke open again. Kenny was on crutches for most of four years, from the time he was seven or eight, and Bob was nine. For weeks at a time, the doctors of Russell had Kenny tied down on the bed the boys shared while they sowed his leg with maggots, to eat away the disease. There were hundreds of them in his leg, gnawing, eating at him all the time. You could hear them! (Like hogs eating corn, Kenny said.) The smell of sickness filled the house. Finally, Kenny was in the hospital at Hays. Bina traveled the thirty miles every day. Doran would come home after work, bathe and eat, then he'd drive his old green Whippet to Hays to join her. If Doran had a dollar saved before Kenny went to Hays, that was the last he saw of it. The other kids would listen at the table while Bina and Doran plotted payments to the doctors, in currency of chickens, or eggs. Bob didn't understand all the finance, but he knew one thing before he was ten: he was never going to be sick like that, never going to cost the family that way. Bobby Joe was going to be the strong one. He was going to be a man.

After he took the job at Dawson's—every day after school and Saturdays—he was, in fact, a little man of the town. Dawson's was the place to go in Russell, for medicine, of course, but also for ice cream, coffee, or just conversation. During the day, Dawson's drew at least one visit from everyone who worked in town. At night, they got everybody from the Mecca Theater, and the Dream, all the kids from the roller rink, the men from the pool hall across the street, shoppers and storeowners who came by after they closed. "Meet you at the drugstore," they'd call to one another across Main Street. When Bob started out, old Dutch Dawson was still in charge, but most days he sat in his back booth and the tone of the place really came from his sons. Ernie Dawson, the oldest, was the quietest: he was the pharmacist, he worked in the back. Chet and Bub Dawson were the ringleaders, working out front, with the sundries, at the fountain, dealing with the folks, giving them "the treatment." If Bub saw a lady crossing Main Street, gingerly pulling the scarf off her new perm, on her way into Dawson's for that new-style curler they'd just recommended while they worked her over at the beauty salon, he'd say, when she walked in patting her coif: "Thought you were goin' to the beauty parlor. . . . They too busy? Couldn't take ya today?" If a man walked in with paint on his pants, Chet might loudly start a collection, dunning all the codgers who did crosswords under the ceiling fans at the wooden-top tables for "a nickel apiece t'get ol' Ben some clean pants." That was if the fellow didn't really need the nickels. It got so people stuck their heads in just to get their insult for the day. Most came in and stayed for a while, listening to Chet's constant plaint about his wife, "ornery, damn fool woman . . ."

It didn't take Bob long to catch on. He had Doran's gift of deadpan humor and, soon, he had his own patter for the public. For his schoolmates, he learned to flip the ice cream or the cherry into the air, before it landed in the mixing cup, or the glass, where he'd pour the soda on top. "Nickel green river, comin' up," he'd announce, then ask: "You want the flip in it?" He talked to the adults who took their coffee breaks on the fountain stools, and he could retail all the news in town. People thought nothing of asking young Bob what happened with that wreck on the highway last night. And Chet or Bub'd call across the store: "Why you askin' Bob? He's just the soda jerk." And Bob'd snap back: "Well, somebody had to have the intelligence to mix a milkshake 'round here."

Such a little man of the town!

Such a man at school! Most of the kids who left Russell High at three o'clock each afternoon wouldn't see a thing until they came back the next day: it was home, supper, homework, maybe Jack Benny or the Lone Ranger on the family radio. But Bob was in town every night. He knew who ducked into the back room at Dawson's, where they might put something extra in their Cokes. He saw the men stopping by the newsstand next to the theater where they had two slot machines, and the woman who ran it was a whore! Heck, he'd been in the pool hall! Donny Sellens's pool hall was a place kids didn't go. But Donny had a lunch counter in there, and when Bob worked a full day, Saturdays or summers, he was allowed to walk right in. He only got fifteen minutes for lunch, and Sellens's was just across the street. He'd climb onto a stool and they wouldn't have to ask: Bob got the quarter special, a hot dog, bowl of chili, and a Coke. They'd shove a box of crackers and a bottle of ketchup down the counter, and he'd eat all the crackers, and pour all the ketchup into his chili. Meanwhile, he'd watch the tables. That was as close as he ever got: pretty innocent, when you got down to it. But when Bob went back to school, all he had to say to draw an openmouthed stare was "Guess who I saw in the pool hall . . ."

There were plenty of places kids didn't go when Bob was growing up. After oil was discovered (in '23, the year Bob was born) under a knoll on the prairie west of town, the highways into Russell were studded with neon—at least for the boom years of the twenties. By the Sheriff's count, there were twenty-seven nightclubs and honky-tonks: the Pineboard, Lindy's, Jack's Shack, and Geibel's Gables, out about fifteen miles north of town at Highway K-18; the Cotton Club, out by the stock-yards, the Lakeside, the Big Apple, the Sunflower, the Red Star, out on Highway 40 East. . . . The bar rum was bootleg, there were slots, dice tables, blackjack, poker rooms. Women were expensive, in short supply. Drew Pearson passed through town in the 1930s, and wrote it up as "Little Chicago."

Well, anyway, it was little. In the twenties, Russell couldn't grow fast enough. The first handful of roughnecks who came in from Wichita, Tulsa, Oklahoma City, filled up the hotel and a couple of boardinghouses. The later ones ended up sleeping in garages, attics, and chicken coops. They were rough boys, too. The shopkeepers on Main Street called them Oklahoma Rounders—when you'd ask where they came from, they'd an-swer, "Aw, 'round Oklahoma." If they got work, they'd spend their weeks in cabin camps out on the prairie, slinging mud, hefting pipe. Then they'd get paid and you'd see them in their new clothes, strutting to the pool hall on Saturday night. When there wasn't work, some of them hung around Main Street, scorned as "oil trash" by the good women of Russell. If they got flat broke, they worked half-days, unloading cement at the rail-road siding: that was hard labor, twenty cents an hour. But that was money in Russell, especially in the thirties, when the boom went bust.

People in Russell used to say, with an odd sort of pride, that there wasn't any family in town that hadn't been broke, one time or another. There just wasn't any money around. When the roughnecks showed up at Dawson's, got some ice cream, and slapped down a ten-dollar bill, Bob had to run to the bank to get change. When the oilmen's kids showed up at the grade school with shiny new bikes—brand-new twenty-five-dollar bikes!— local kids couldn't believe it. In Russell, you'd trade a bike for $2.50, and you might save for a year to get that. There was a lot of resentment on Main Street. And it could have got bitter on Maple, too, when Bina announced to the children that they could put their things down in the basement. Everything: clothes, schoolbooks, family pictures! The whole family was moving to the basement. *Get your things downstairs! Right now!* . . . Doran would rig a bathtub for washing and a hot plate for Bina to cook on. He'd rented the house to some oilmen: hundred dollars a month, cash in advance, for a year! That was twelve hundred dollars, cash money! . . . That night, Doran stayed out on the porch so late, the kids thought he was waiting for the bank to open.

Bob stayed awake that night, too. But he never said a word about it. Never called anybody "oil trash." Never had a bad word for anybody. Wouldn't spend the time on it, for one thing. No, he had plans of his own. For a start, he was saving for a new bike. It'd cost twenty-six dollars, but he figured all four Dole kids could use it. They could get a paper route, and that would make the money back, maybe help out at home.

Bob always had a plan. It was funny how that kind of will sprang up in a place where plans were so fragile. Back when the railroad first arrived, the town fathers had it in mind that Russell would rival Kansas City as the hub of commerce for the plains. Doran's dad was going to buy more land, before the bad years hit, one after the other, and he lost his own quarter-section. And did Doran have dreams for the White Front Café? If he did, he didn't bring them up anymore. In Russell, it was best not to talk about your hopes, past or present. Better just to make a joke, and move on. Put your head down, work for a living. That was hard enough, in the thirties—especially when the dust came.

When the dust storms hit, the sky would grow black in the southwest and the light would disappear as if a curtain were drawn across the prairie. They'd run to get the kids out of school. Kids were dying from the dust pneumonia. They had to wrap the babies in wet sheets, so they wouldn't suffocate from the dirt in the air.

Bob'd run home, and Kenny would come stumping behind, to fill the bathtub and soak the towels and pack them around the windows and doors, trying to keep the dust out. But there wasn't any way to stop it. You had to wash everything in the house so you could eat. If you left a bowl of water overnight, it'd be muddy by morning. You couldn't see the pattern on the kitchen linoleum. On the west side of town, where the Doles lived, they scooped dirt out of houses with wheat shovels.

After '33, when it pretty much quit raining for the next few years, the dust was the overwhelming fact of life. In town, they'd turn on the streetlights, and people would feel their way home, walking next to the curbs. In Hays, they had a basketball game, and they had to stop to sweep the floor every ten minutes. They couldn't see the lines on the court. Anyway, the Hays coliseum was lit with skylights, and after a while, they couldn't see to play, but they wouldn't let anybody leave, either. They'd be lost out there in the dust.

Out on the land, the dust would cover the fence posts, drift up to the top of a barn. You'd see a pipe sticking up from the dirt, and you knew a tractor got caught in the dust.

The trees died. The grass died. Land was selling for five dollars an acre, if you could find a buyer. One farmer, up in Gorham, went to the bank and they turned him down, so he herded his cattle to a corner of the fence and he shot them, one by one . . . and then he shot himself. In Russell, one of the Krug boys lost his hope somehow, and hung himself in his bedroom. Doc White went over, but all he could do was hold him while his daughters cut him down.

Jack Phipps, who had a place on Kansas Street, got the dust pneumonia. The men of the Russell Volunteer Fire Department stood in front of Jack's house for days, doing shifts with a hose, in darkness and light, couple hours at a stretch, spraying water over Jack's house, trying to keep the dust off. Doran was there, of course. He was a volunteer fireman for fifty-one years. He took his turn with the hose at Jack's house. Seemed like every man in town did. But there wasn't any way to keep the dust out. Jack Phipps died, right there in that house.

Bob Dole knew all that. Lord, in Russell, there wasn't any way not to know. But that wasn't him. His life was going to be different. And it wasn't any dream, either. It was a plan. He worked on it every day, how he was going to make it happen.

———————

At 10:00 P.M., old Dutch Dawson would look up at the clock from the back booth of the drugstore, where he was doing his crossword, with his glasses on top of his head. He'd lift his squat frame out of the booth and walk to the front door. He'd look up Main Street, then down the other way. "Wait a minute. Don't turn the lights out," he'd say. "There's a guy comin' out of the theater. . . . Okay, turn 'em out. He went the other way."

Then, he'd check the two registers at the front, the sundries and the fountain, turn the key, and check the ring-up. Then, he'd get into his car, and head home.

The boys and Bob stayed behind, cleaning up. Bob had to make syrup for the next day, empty the ice-cream bins, wash out the soda spigots . . . those things had to be clean. It was always closer to eleven when he ran back to Maple Street. Bina would have his supper waiting. And not just a plate of something on the stove, but his place set at the dining room table, homemade bread, soup, a full dinner. There was fresh cake or pie for dessert. Bina's girls, Bob's two sisters, had to bake a fresh dessert when they got home from school. There was no halfway, or good-enough, with Bina Dole.

People used to say there was nothing Bina couldn't get done. But it had to be done just so. It didn't matter how much effort it took, or how many hours. When Bob's older sister, Gloria, started to iron, and a shirt wasn't just so, Bina'd throw that shirt right back on the pile. "Sista! . . ." (That was Gloria's nickname.) "You have to learn to do things right!" She'd have Gloria, or her youngest child, Norma Jean, standing for hours on a dining room chair, while she got the hem of a skirt just right. "Stand *still!* . . ." When Bina set to cleaning floors, all four kids had to get up on those chairs, and woe to the child who jumped the gun and put a foot down on the damp floor. "You can go out back and cut your switch, right now!" (Bina's voice could take paint off a wall: even her name rasped with hard prairie vowels; it rhymed with Carolina, or, as she'd likely say, Salina.)

Around Eleventh and Maple, the neighbors would hear her make those kids hop: "Bob, you sweep off that porch! Kenny! You get that trash together!" Or she'd call down to the grain elevator, light into Doran so hard that the farmers having coffee could hear her on Doley's end of the line. *This was wrong and that was wrong, and if Doran didn't care, well, that was just too bad!* Then she'd slam down the phone without saying goodbye. Doran would just put down the phone and go about his business; he was used to Bina; he toed the mark, best he could. One time, they had a family reunion, and what with all the Talbotts (Bina came from a family of twelve kids), they had to use the second floor of the community hall. Well, it was Doran's job to set up the tables, and Doran being the way he was, he went the extra mile, got some paper tablecloths, and set all the places— plates and silverware, too. So Bina walked in, and she hit the roof! "Well, my GOD, Doran! Get those papers off the tables! I've got tablecloths and we're SURE not gonna eat on those papers!" Doran just went back and took it all apart. "Well," he said, quietly, shaking his head, stripping tables, "I knew there'd be somethin' wrong. I was just wonderin' what it would be."

She didn't demand anything from them that she wouldn't do herself. She was surely the only woman in Russell who'd scrub down her wooden front porch, and then wax it. She'd wax and shine the garbage cans! She had the five rooms on Maple Street done up like a dollhouse, with organdy curtains she made herself. The girls had party dresses she made, with ruffles, all perfectly turned and ironed. And snappy pleated jumpers for their Legion Auxiliary uniforms: Bina made them, too. She'd cut down her old coats to make their coats. Each of the boys had only one set of school clothes, but they were immaculate every day, trousers creased, shirts pressed. Every day, there was a clean white shirt and white cotton pants, ironed just so, for work at the drugstore. Doran got a fresh white shirt every day, and fresh overalls, ironed smooth. Everything, even sheets and dish towels, had to be ironed, and just so. On wash day, Monday, there were four or five lines in the yard.

That's the way Bina learned when she was a girl on the Talbott farm. Joseph and Elva Talbott were reckoned the handsomest couple in the county, and at their place, a dozen miles south of Russell, everything had to be just so. Joseph used to mow the verge of the road, county land, so the weeds wouldn't spoil the look of his farm. He was so particular about his horses, he'd wash their hooves. There were eight daughters and four sons, and as Joseph was a member of the district school board, they generally had the schoolmistress boarding with them, too. The Talbotts did their own milking, they raised their own chickens, cleaned 'em and picked 'em for Sunday dinner. There were seven ponies for the kids to ride, Sunday afternoons. Monday was for washing, Tuesday for ironing, Wednesday was mending and altering, Thursday was housecleaning, Friday and Saturday they baked. When they'd get up, two boys and three girls would milk four cows apiece. After school, some of the kids would gather eggs. Some of the girls had to wash the dishes. There was a pump in the kitchen and they'd fill the kettle, boil the water for scalding. The stove had a reservoir: hot water for cleaning. They all had to pick up their rooms and make their beds before they could come down to breakfast. The evening meal was the big event. Tablecloth and silver every night. Elva's kids didn't have to be told to be cleaned up and ready in their chairs.

When Bina married Doran and got her own house, that was the way she ran it, too. In the years before Bobby Joe went to work at the drugstore (and Kenny after him, a couple of years later), everybody had to be home and cleaned up for dinner. Before suppertime, the boys would go downstairs to light the water heater. ("Your dad's comin' home. He'll want to clean up.")

Then, to the dining room: tablecloth, every night. The Dole kids would climb into their seats, hands washed, faces washed, hair combed. Doran would fix the children's plates. And every night, he'd say: "Dessert's under your plate." That meant no pie till they ate all he gave them. After dinner and the dishes, all the kids did their homework at the dining room table. *The Salina Journal* came by train every evening, and Doran read it at night, in his chair in the front room, next to the round-top Philco. Saturdays, Doran had his radio shows: *Fibber McGee and Mollie, Amos 'n' Andy.* The kids could go out after supper Saturdays, but they got themselves home on time. Last thing they wanted was to make Dad leave the Philco, go out hunting kids, in the middle of *Amos 'n' Andy.* Sunday nights, after the dishes, they'd make a plate of fudge. One of the girls got to make it, the other kids would sit and watch, so nobody got to lick more. They had their fudge, and their baths. Bina would hand out the soap. "No one's so poor they can't buy soap . . ." Then it was all kids to bed, all in the back bedroom. There was a bed for the boys and one for the girls. (Later, when the kids were teenagers, Doran fixed up a boys' room in the concrete basement.) Bina or Doran would turn out the light, and that was that: time to sleep.

Even when Bob was coming home late, Bina would still be working: ironing in the kitchen, or sewing in the dining room, at her place near the south window. Sometimes, she'd sew till four in the morning, finishing something for the girls, or something special for a customer. Bina was a working mother, a rare breed in those days: she sold Singer sewing machines in the Russell district. She'd drive the country roads, sometimes fifty miles out of town, hauling her big machine in the back of her old Chevy, where Doran took out the rumble seat. Then with two trips back and forth from the car, she'd lug the machine into a farmhouse (first the heavy steel head, then the base and the treadle), and set it up to demonstrate. She'd grab whatever fabric they had—anything, a feed sack—and turn out a dress right there. Or she'd show the machine, and then, at home, stay up into the night, making a dress, or pleated curtains, for the lady of that house, where she'd show up again, next day:

"You know, I was thinking about you last night, and I decided to make . . ." And she'd give her work to the woman and assure her it was nothing, no trouble at all. It was easy, with a Singer machine. . . .

Sometimes, the kids would get home after school to find Bina out at work. The house would be studded with notes:

Do the dishes.

Put the potatoes in at 4:00.

Then, just before Doran got home, Bina's Chevy would roar up Eleventh Street (she always drove foot-to-the-floorboard, till she got where she was going), and Bina would lug the machine back into the house, along with a fistful of chickens, a couple of pounds of aluminum, or a pound of copper. . . . She'd take anything that she could convert to $1.75, the down payment on a Singer. That night, she'd be up late again, catching up on her mending, or baking, or working on her next sewing project.

There was never enough time in the day, never any time for dreaming. "If you shirk work," Bina told her kids, "work shirks you." That's what her grandmother used to say. There wasn't any point telling Bina, "I can't . . ." That was one thing she wouldn't abide. There wasn't anything Bina couldn't get done, and there wasn't anything they couldn't do, if they were willing to work at it. "Can't never could do nothin'!" she'd say. "Now, get busy!"

The only time she wasn't doing four things at once was

when the headaches came upon her. It was only every so
often—sometimes a year would go by without—but when they
came, even a footstep on the floor hurt. Bina would shut herself
into the front bedroom, sometimes for days. Doran would get up
earlier to fix breakfast for the kids, and he'd be home at midday,
too, to get lunch ready, and send them back to school. But there
was nothing anyone could really do for Bina. God knows, Doran
would have leapt to do anything. It was such a helpless feeling
in the house. One time, in the middle of the night, Bina must
have said something about milk. Doran jumped up from his
sleep and woke Bob: Your mother wants some milk! Bob went
straight to the grocery, and only then did Doran look at a clock.
It was three in the morning. There was nothing open in Russell.
When Bob didn't come back, after an hour, Doran went to hunt
him. He found him half-asleep, eyes puffed and drooping
closed, sitting on the curb in front of Holzer's grocery, waiting
for the shop to open.

Bob took it to heart when Bina was sick with her headaches. There was an understanding, a shared set of standards
between those two. Sometimes she used to tell her sisters,
Bobby Joe was more particular than she was. One time she
found him with a sweater on in the middle of summer.

"Bob, aren't you hot? Bob! Take that sweater off!"

No, he said, it was all right.

When she asked him again, she found out: his shirt was
wrinkled. He didn't want that to show.

When he got older, sometimes he'd pay his sisters a nickel
to iron his shirt. But it had to be ironed just so. He was worse
than Bina. That was the way he held himself, in every thing he
did. In a gaggle of kids outside the high school, you would always notice Bob, always with a crowd around him. Bob was the

tallest, and he held himself perfectly straight. Of course, he was scrubbed and combed, with his thick dark hair in perfect trim. Lord knows, the girls noticed: in his senior year, the members of the Girls Reserve voted Bob Dole their Ideal Boy. But that wasn't why Bob did all that. He didn't have time for girls. He was just working on himself.

Bob had the first set of weights in Russell, an iron bar with blocks of cement on either end. He used to lift that thing every chance he got, until he was thick with muscle. By the end of high school, he was six-foot-one, 192 pounds, with legs that could pull like a tractor. Building his body was part of the program.

He never walked anywhere, but ran. God hadn't really blessed him with speed, but he worked at it, and he made himself a runner, held a local record in the half-mile, and beat some college boys from Hays while he was still in high school.

That was only one of his sports. He won three letters at Russell High. In the fall, he played on the football team, as an end, a pass receiver, although under Coach Baxter's single wing, there weren't too many passes to catch. George Baxter preached a brand of drive-'em-back, knock-'em-down football that relied more on stamina and will than grace. In fact, Coach did more than preach. If a boy didn't hit the way Coach wanted, then Coach would drop to a three-point stance and knock the kid on his ass. (No pads in those days, either.) He never had to do that with Bobby Dole. Bob and Bud Smith, best friends, were leaders on the team. Bud was one of the oil kids, came to Russell in '37. Bob and Bud were the best athletes. In any game, they were Russell High's one-two punch.

But in basketball, Bob Dole was the leader, the big guy on the court. In team huddles, he was the one to go around, clap every man on the backside, tell him they could win, *had* to win. "Don't give up, guys. We're gonna get 'em," he'd say. "We still got a chance. They can go sour." If things went badly, you could see his eyes tearing up and he'd turn away, go off by himself. He never told anyone, but he used to dream about basketball, how he'd make the baskets, how Russell would win. And the basketball Broncos were winners. Got to the state tournament one year. You had to be good to make that team. Bobby Dole was good. He could handle the ball, shoot that newfangled one-hand push shot, and he was big and tough under the boards.

It wasn't just his size, it was his attitude, conditioning . . . and the game itself was changing. Up until 1937, there was a jump ball after every basket. The game would stop, as the boys arrayed themselves anew at center court. But that year, just as Bob made the Russell High team, the rules changed. When one team made a basket, the other team got the ball. Suddenly, there were no breaks. For a boy like Bob, who could run all day, who *did* run all day, it was the best change possible. He was always in the middle of the action. He brought the ball up, saw the whole court. He set up the play, made it happen. When it came time to pick the Union Pacific All-Stars, the best from the towns along the railroad trunk line, Bob Dole was the only Russell boy picked by the coaches of the conference.

Basketball was the game Russell watched. Kansas was basketball country, and had been for years, ever since the University of Kansas brought in the game's inventor, James Naismith, as the chief of athletics. Naismith trained the coaches who fanned out to towns around the state—and to colleges around the country. One legend of the modern game, Adolph Rupp, the revered coach of Kentucky, played his ball at KU for Naismith. So did the next legend of Kansas basketball, Forrest C. "Phog"

Allen, so nicknamed for his stentorian voice, who was the KU coach while Bob grew up, and a godly figure all over the state.

In Russell, KU had the air of the East, of money and sophistication. Snob Hill, they called it. If Phog had ever walked down Main Street, there wasn't anyone in Russell who wouldn't have stopped work, and run to the window to look. As it was, you couldn't get your hair cut or your car fixed on the afternoon of a local high school game. The gym was the newest, biggest building in town, and everybody was there. You had to go early and sit through the "B" game (for kids who couldn't quite make the grade) to have your place at seven o'clock, for the "A" game. By four or four-thirty, the men and boys would get their afternoon papers and a sack of sandwiches and head over to the gym. The women showed up later with their knitting. By midnight, there wasn't anyone in Russell who didn't know how the Broncos did, and half the town probably stopped at Dawson Drug to discuss it.

That's one of the reasons Bob got the job at Dawson's. The Dawson boys wanted a kid for that fountain job who was a leader, who'd bring in the other kids. Bob Dole, basketball star, was that boy. Anyway, there were no bigger fans in town than Chet and Bub Dawson. (Chet was a diehard K-State fan. He'd claim: "If KU was playin' Russia, I'd root for Russia.")

That was the same reason Bob got the Kaw Pipeline job. Every summer, the pipeline company gave one job to a high school kid, and that was the best job in town, the biggest money a kid could make. Usually, the job went to the best athlete. The oil companies sponsored semipro teams, and there were more than a few oil workers whose main job was playing in the weekly games. In fact, the year Bob got the job, one of those workers was Phog Allen's kid, Milton (they called him Mitt), who had better moves on the gym floor than he did around an oil rig. That's when Bob Dole's plan came together, when the pieces clicked into place.

Bob wanted to go to college. He'd kept his eyes open at Dawson's and he'd seen who it was who never seemed to want, the men everybody listened to, men of substance, respect. They were the doctors, whose word was law in any drugstore. So Bob was going to be a doctor: he was going to get to college, and then to med school. And when that was done, he'd have made it, past the dreams of any kid from Russell, past any insecurity, reach of fortune, weather, dust, or want.

But how? No one named Dole had the money for a year of college, much less seven. Then Phog Allen came to visit his son. And Mitt Allen told his dad that he ought to meet this boy named Dole, who was a heck of a nice guy, and a heck of a ballplayer, too. Phog Allen himself came into the drugstore! And shook Bob's hand! And later that year, Bob got a note from the East, from Lawrence, from KU, Snob Hill! *Bob Dole got a letter from Phog Allen himself!*

See, it wasn't a dream, after all! Bob Dole was going to KU. He was going to play for Phog Allen. They gave scholarships to the team, didn't they? It could be done!

Harold Dumler, from Russell, he was a few years older, he made it to KU. Heck, he was already rushing Bob Dole for Kappa Sigma! *Bob Dole had a letter from Phog Allen!*

When the boys from Kappa Sig made their rush tour in the summer, it was Bob Dole who put on the party for them in Russell. It was real! Harold said Bob could wait tables at the Kappa Sig house. He could pay his board that way.

Bob talked to Bina. He said he wouldn't go if it would be too hard on her and Dad. He knew things were tight. He knew how hard they worked. But Bina said he'd better go. Can't never could do nothin', she said. They'd find money, if it came to that.

And there was nothing Bina couldn't get done. When Bob got the train east in September, she sent him with sixty-five dollars, cash.

1945

Bob Dole didn't want to go to war. He was doing what he wanted, at KU, in the Kappa Sig house, doing what he never had time to do before: fooling around.

He was just ornery enough to be a good pledge. There was a pledge brother with a motorcycle, a big old Harley, weighed about a *ton*. Bob and some of the others hauled that bike up to a third-floor bedroom, then wouldn't help the fellow bring it down. That sealed Bob's fame. He even sailed through the hazing. Hell Week, the "actives" made freshmen wear burlap underwear to class. Bob laughed that off. The older guys got staves from a barrel factory, to whack the pledges into line. Bob said, "I've heard so much about those boards, I better find out how bad it's gonna be." So he made one of the actives haul off and whack him—hard as he could. Pretty near drove him through the wall. Bob said, "Well, that wasn't so bad." That was the last time anybody hit him.

He was going out for football, basketball, and track, so he kept up his training. He asked a friend coming from Russell to bring his concrete weights in her car. And he kept up his running, every day, before the others were awake. He was waiting tables in the house to pay his dues, and he had a milk route, dawn Saturdays, that earned him pocket money. A Big Man on Campus, like Bob Dole intended to be, had to have money to spend. . . . Grace McCandless was the most beautiful girl on campus, and Bob Dole, freshman, invited her home for Christmas. (Bina was so excited, she baked twice as many cookies.) Before he left in December, Bob was elected vice president of Kappa Sigma. In his first term! But with all the new things he was trying that year, something had to slip: his grade point slid below the gentleman's C, and he couldn't make initiation. He was still a pledge in December, when the Japanese bombed Pearl Harbor, and Bob Dole's bright new world started to change.

He hung on at KU as long as he could. Heck, people said the war might be over before they got to him. He ran track that spring, finished the school year and started another. He played another season of football, then basketball, and more than a year after Pearl Harbor, Bob was still at school. But it got to be obvious that every man was going. Pretty soon his draft board would turn up his number—they were already coming for Kenny, back in Russell—so Bob looked to his chances, and signed up for the Army Enlisted Reserve Corps. That way, at least he'd get to finish the term.

What did he know about the war in Europe? KU, in Lawrence, was the farthest east he'd ever been. When the Army called him in '43, and sent him off to basic training, they gave him his first plane ride. Heck, his first bus ride! Turned out, Bob and Kenny ended up in basic at the same time, the summer of '43, at Camp Barkley, near Abilene, Texas. So Bina bought herself a train ticket, and showed up at the base, blew past the sentry: What was he going to do, shoot her? Bina marched down the dusty main street of camp, looking for her boys. The MPs tried to talk her into leaving, but she'd have none of it. "I've got two boys here and I've come to visit." They had to call the camp commandant to deal with her. "Ma'am, you cannot go walking around here. If you'll just wait, we'll get your boys for you."

But soon, they were far out of her reach. Kenny was shipped to the Pacific. Bob signed up for Army Engineering School, in the strange new world of Brooklyn, New York. After that, he was transferred to Camp Polk, Louisiana, then to Camp Breckenridge, in Kentucky, for antitank gunnery. By the spring of 1944, he'd made corporal and applied for officer training. The news from Europe was better and better: the U.S. was marching up the boot of Italy, Mussolini was out of power. As Bob Dole reported to Fort Benning, Georgia, for his three-month Officer Candidate School, the Allies were fighting their way off the beaches in Normandy. By the time he got his lieutenancy, Paris was free, the Germans were pulling back.... Who could tell if he'd get there in time to fire a shot?

There was time. The invasions of Europe had taken a fearful toll among the junior officers who led platoons. By December 1944, Bob Dole was headed east, across the Atlantic. It was just before Christmas when he pitched up outside Rome, where the Army maintained a replacement camp, from which to deal out officers to plug the gaps in its ranks.

———————

The first thing everyone noticed about Bob Dole was his strength. He was six-foot-two, a hundred ninety-four pounds. Then, too, he always wore a tank jacket that gave his upper body more bulk. The guy was big as a house. In fact, his body almost kept him out of the fighting. In Rome, he ran into Dean Nesmith, the trainer for Phog Allen's KU teams. Nesmith was a taskmaster, an ex-football hero with a prognathous jaw, and no tolerance for whiners or weaklings. Now he was in the Army's Special Services unit: sports and games for the guys behind the lines. He knew Dole, liked him: Bob was a kid who'd never quit. So he tried to get Dole into his outfit, as one of the trainers, a coach for the troops.

But too late: the Army had milled out orders for Dole to fill a slot with the Eighty-fifth Mountain Regiment, Third Battalion. The mountain troops were fighting their way up the spine of Italy, in a drive to the broad Po Valley, and beyond, to the Alps, to cut off the Germans before they could fall back to reinforce the Reich. At least, that was the plan: like most things in Italy, nothing went according to plan. The whole Italian invasion was a sop to Stalin, who demanded a second front in 1943. The U.S. went along, but insisted that no men or matériel be diverted from the next year's grand D-Day plunge. Meanwhile, Hitler annexed Italy and ordered his generals there to fight to the last drop of blood. The result was the war's most vicious sideshow: a meat grinder of a year and a half, where America lost tens of thousands of men, chewing north at less than a mile a day, in a campaign that history would little remark. Among the original 200 men of the company to which Dole was assigned, there were 183 casualties in four months after they debarked in Naples. When Dole got his orders, in February '45, the battalion had just fought its first major engagement: a night assault on Mt. Belvedere; in less than twenty-four hours, a company commander and half the lieutenants were gone.

Of course, Dole didn't know all that. In Uncle Sam's infantry, you were lucky to know what was going on a hundred yards to your right or left. But he knew, somehow, it was bad business up there: he told Dean Nesmith he didn't want to go. He sensed there was a bullet waiting for him in those hills. Nesmith told him to pack his kit. There was nothing more to be said.

———

That was the other thing they noticed about Dole, when he got to the mountains and took over Second Platoon: the way he held himself so quiet, like he'd stepped into someone else's war, and didn't want to intrude. He wasn't like some of those ninety-day wonders, graduates of the Benning School for Boys, who thought they owned the world because they got a strip of brass on their collars. Dole knew what it meant to be a lieutenant of infantry: he was fodder, the guy out front, the guy with the binoculars and map case, whom the Jerries tried to shoot first because it would disrupt the chain of command. German snipers went for the officers and radio men: if they got them, the unit was cut off, disorganized, without eyes and ears. . . . Of course, every man in the unit knew that: Dole could see the way they looked him over—coolly, like they didn't want to invest too much, he might not be around for long. "I'm Lieutenant Dole," he'd say, introducing himself. "I'm going to be leading the platoon. . . ." If they didn't say anything, he'd add: "Dole. Like the pineapple juice."

A sergeant, Frank Carafa, was in charge of the platoon when Dole arrived. (Their lieutenant had moved up when the company commander was killed on Mt. Belvedere.) Carafa was small, quick, dark-eyed, a veteran; he'd been in the Army before the war, fought in the Pacific before he joined the mountain troops. Dole asked him how long he'd been running the platoon. Carafa looked him over: the wide boyish eyes under his helmet (guy was so green, he still wore his helmet!), the big tank jacket with pockets everywhere, the pants wrapped tight around his legs and tucked neatly into the top of his boots, the clean kit on the ground beside him . . . straight off the boat.

"Since Belvedere," he said.

"All right, soldier. There won't be any changes," Dole said. "We'll run it like you've been running it, until we get the knack of it."

Carafa nodded, and his eyes met Dole's for a moment.

———————

He was scared twenty-four hours a day. Hell, everybody was. The Germans were giving ground, hill by hill, and when the Americans fought their way onto the next peak, the Jerries knew every inch of that position. They knew where the cover was: they could zero in their artillery, the .88s—and they were good. Carafa used to say they could hit a fly in the tail, while it flew. "Mail'll be in about five," the men would remind each other grimly. That meant artillery rounds, day after day, dawn and dusk, sometimes all night in the dark. So they dug in—fox-holes, twenty-four hours a day, two men on their stomachs in the cold stony ground, one staring off at the facing hillside, watching the Germans through a twenty-power scope (sometimes, they were so close, you could spot their snipers from a puff of rifle smoke), the other trying to get his two hours' sleep, until it was his turn to wake and watch. Food came from cans in their kits: spaghetti and meatballs, or beef stew; you didn't dare make a fire to heat it.

There were daily rumors of a breakout, the big push that

would carry them over the ridges and into the Po Valley. It was coming, and soon. Everybody knew it. In fact, the brass had the plans drawn up, the race for the bridges over the Po, and then for the Alps, to cut off the Germans. The generals called it Operation Craftsman; but no one on the line knew the code name. Bellied to the stones in a shell hole, they worried about the guys in the next hole, six feet away. Were they still there? . . . Were there Jerries out front? . . . The goddam fog was the worst. You didn't know who was around you.

It was scariest for the replacements, guys who never bargained for infantry. Most were "Triple-A," antiaircraft artillerymen who'd been sitting in Rome. But the Luftwaffe was finished now, so they handed these poor bastards a rifle and a shovel, and stuck 'em in foxholes. One guy they stuck in Dole's platoon was mental with the fear. Dev Jennings, one of the sergeants, went to the company command post to tell 'em they better have a look at the guy. "He's just not gonna be with us." But just as Jennings brought the exec to the guy's foxhole, they heard a shot—M-1, an American—and they found the kid standing in a corner, where he'd braced against the sides of the hole to keep still, while he fired a bullet from his rifle through his left foot. He was still holding his M-1 in position, with a blank stare on his face. They shipped him off to the aid station, wrote it up: gunshot, self-inflicted. What else could they do?

⸻

They were supposed to start the breakout April 12, with Dole's company on the left flank, to take a rocky, brown, flattop hill, Number 913 on the maps, to clear the way for the drive to the Po. Dole got his orders as he always did, face-to-face, a visit from the company commander. There were no ready rooms for the grunts, no meetings called on that front. Why get a half-dozen officers together, where one mortar shell could take them out?

Dole's platoon, about forty men, was supposed to stay on the left, moving down their slope and then across a thousand yards of shallow valley, over a short stone fence, and up the slope of Hill 913. Everybody knew the Jerries were dug in all over that hill: pillboxes with tunnels between them. The Jerries knew the ground like they'd farmed it for forty years. They knew where a squad leader in the field would eye a spot of welcome cover: that's where they'd strew their mines and booby traps, or zero in their .81 mortars, ahead of time. It was Dole's job to keep his guys out of those spots, to belly through that field, dodging everything the Krauts could throw, to bring his guys to the top of that hill, or as many guys as he had left: that was the awful calculus behind the brave word "breakout." How much ground did he have to take? How many of his guys would get the mattress-cover on the way?

They were Dole's guys now. A month is a long time in foxholes under fire. His tank jacket didn't look so new. Now he kept extra clips of ammo taped together, like the vets, to give him forty-five quick rounds. He knew enough to keep a few grenades on his belt, no matter what the book said about leaving that to the men. The first grenade he threw bounced off a tree in the dark and blew up just a few yards away. He could still feel where a piece of hot metal flew into his leg. When was that—last month? Ancient history. Now, in the dark before the attack, Dole went down the line to his guys, a word for each, to see they were ready, a pat on the back . . .

Funny thing about that. You go down a line of grunts before dawn of a big day, give 'em a pat, and just about every one—to a man—he'll fart. They've got their rifles clean, they've counted their grenades, their bullets, checked all their lucky little things, and then there's nothing to do, except get tight inside. Then you come and pat 'em on the ass. . . . In the Army, they call it the pucker factor. It was high that day.

But the goddam fog stopped the plan. The bombers were coming, to soften up the Krauts, but they couldn't take off from their fields near Pisa. So all the guys could do was lie back and wait. Then, that day, FDR died. The news came, foxhole to foxhole. Some men took it hard. Not that it changed what they had to do. It was just another reminder: the war was almost over, everybody knew . . . but the old man didn't make it. Would they? . . . They waited another day.

On the morning of the fourteenth, the weather cleared, the bombers came. It was bombing like the guys in Italy had never seen: wave after wave of planes, hitting the hillsides with five-hundred pounders . . . then the heavy artillery zeroed in on the same hills for another hour. The noise was incredible, and the guys were grinning. "God, boy, they sure ain't alive in there now."

"No fuckin' way!"

By the time the bombardment stopped, near 10:00 A.M., no one could see Hill 913. The air was opaque with smoke and dust, the world was dark with brown grit, as the word went down the line and the boys scrambled out of their holes and Bob Dole went ahead, into the valley, into the dust.

———————

But the Germans were alive, hundreds of them. April 14 was a daytime nightmare of cannon, mortar, machine-gun fire—flesh in uneven contest with the "instrumentalities of war." A second lieutenant named Kvam tried to take cover from artillery, dived into a shallow ditch, and tripped a Kraut booby trap. It was a steel pipe, cut on a diagonal and filled with explosives, so when it blew, it would spray burning steel in a wide, deadly swath. But Kvam took the whole load. When his men got to the hole, it looked like someone had dabbed the lieutenant a hundred times on his face and body with a tiny black paint brush. He was perforated.

Dole got his men down to the low stone wall, and started to advance in British formation. The lead squad, maybe fourteen men, followed two scouts at the point of advance. Two smaller squads were behind on the flanks. Farther behind, at the rear point of the diamond, came the weapons squad, with machine guns and light mortars. The top sergeant would move in the middle, as a belly-crawling, rolling headquarters. Dole could have stayed in the middle, too. But he knew his job, and he did it. He was out front, with the lead squad.

They were pinned down quick. The whole company didn't make a quarter mile that morning. Third Platoon got over the wall, but the sergeant told the men to advance across the field before they'd got engineers to check for mines. So the men of the Third made about forty yards and started stepping on mines. Some were killed right there, many wounded. The rest were pinned down in the field, when a farmhouse on the left opened fire: a Jerry machine-gun nest, sure as shit; the men in the field were hamburger.

Dole had to get that machine gun. The lead squad was going to have to flank that house and get that nest of Krauts. Sergeant Carafa assumed he'd be going out with the squad, but Dole said, "Sergeant, I'll take 'em." Carafa stayed behind to cover. He got the rest of the guys in position to fire at the farmhouse, then called for mortars, while they opened up with BARs—Browning automatics, the light machine guns.

Dole went ahead on the steep, rocky field. With the morning's bombardment, the mortars, and machine-gun fire, the ground was littered with bits of metal. There were still shells flying in from the slope behind the farmhouse, and German mortars dug in on the backside of the hill. Dole made fifty or sixty feet before they spotted him from the farmhouse, opened up on him and his squad. He yanked the pin from a grenade and lobbed it, but it fell short. Romberg, the first scout, was closer. He half stood to let loose a grenade, but they got him. He fell face forward and his helmet rolled off in front of him. Dole couldn't see the second scout. Jerries might have got him, too. Dole dived for a shell hole, made it, but his runner, Sims, did not, he was down. Dole scrambled from the hole on his belly, slithered out on the pocked dirt, while shells tore the air over him, and he grabbed little Sims by a handful of shirt, dragged him back, but he was deadweight, it was too late . . . and now the Jerry gunners sighted Dole, who was scrambling from his hole . . . had to get out, his guys were getting chewed up there . . . and Dole was on all fours, moving, tearing up his hands on the ground, and then . . . he felt a sharp shock of sting in his back, behind the right shoulder, he twisted in the air and went down on his face in the dirt, he couldn't feel his arms, *they shot off my arms,* he couldn't feel . . . couldn't see, face in the dirt, *can't get up to see, can't lift . . . have to get out of here!*

The others could hear him moaning. Carafa thought he heard Dole calling to *him,* heard it plain between the roar of the guns . . . *Sergeant Caraaafa,* . . . Dole only knew they were dragging him, dragging him back into a gully, a shallow depression, rolling him over . . . the tank jacket was shredded open near the neck and shoulder. You could see into Dole through the jacket, through the shoulder, like a gouged fruit, see down to the core, and they folded the lieutenant's arms on his chest, they had to get out. . . . The sergeants said they were going to push to the right, to the east, where the engineers were tripping mines. There was another company to the east, breaking through the German line. They'd get by the hill and the Krauts to the east. They had to get moving. Dole was just lying there, staring up at them, the look in his eyes a silent plea. He knew they had to get out . . . but how could they leave him?

They called in medics, but two got killed trying to get to Dole. There weren't many medics going to make it that day. That's why Sergeant Kuschik carried morphine. Stan Kuschik was a great, hairy bear of a man, son of a Jewish baker from New York. He did the best he could for Dole, more than orders allowed: he pulled up a kid named Arthur McBryar, a Tennessee boy who'd been in Dole's platoon. Kuschik told McBryar to stay with Dole, even though orders said to leave no able-bodied man behind. Dole was gray, like they get before they die. Kuschik couldn't leave him to die there, alone. Before he got out, Kuschik dug through his kit, gave Dole a shot of morphine. Then he dipped his finger into Dole's shredded jacket, and with Dole's blood traced an "M" on his forehead. That'd let the medics know he'd had a shot—another would kill him, overdose . . . if a medic ever got there . . . if McBryar could spot one . . .

McBryar was scared to death. The medics were never gonna find them, down there, in the ravine. There was cover, but no one'd come. Dole was still right where they left him, on his back with his arms crossed over his chest, still conscious, moaning, trying to talk . . . but he couldn't unclench his teeth. He wasn't cryin' or anything. But McBryar was listening to the guns, couldn't catch what Dole was trying to say. It seemed like forever till that Kraut machine gun quit. Artillery was still comin' in. He tried to keep Dole talking, keep him going, afraid he was gonna give out.

Dole went home. He didn't know where the others were, so he went home, had to get home, wasn't cold anymore, but he could feel the air, fresh, cool on his chest, he better get home, get something on, his sweater. He was running up Maple, bright sunshine, it was so bright cold, and Spitzy was running with him, his little white dog, Spitzy, was back, running with him, going home, and there was the hoop, the basketball rim in the open lot next door, and Dole was driving for the rim, to the hoop, he could feel them trying to keep him away, trying to block him, but he could get to the hoop, he could always get in, get the ball over, get the ball up, over, could always get in, dribble once, turn and go, even if he had to bang in, bang his body, arm on his shoulder up in the air, and he was falling falling never hit the ground, falling into dark darker cold he could still feel the arm air cold on him shoving him down, down, and the bright was going, pulling away, and he was falling, couldn't see home or Spitzy, *SPITZY!* . . .

McBryar had a bandage pressed onto Dole's wound, had to try to slow the bleeding. Blood was soaking his jacket and uniform, turning the dry ground dark underneath. "How bad is it?" Dole said through his teeth. McBryar pulled the bandage away. Whatever hit Dole had ripped into everything. McBryar could look into him, see right down to Dole's back. His arm was connected by a couple or three white stringy . . . *Jesus, they blowed his arm off.*

McBryar pressed the bandage down again. "You gonna be fine, Lieutenant."

McBryar cradled Dole's head, gave him the soldier's mix of sulfa and water, trying to hold off infection. He rubbed water on Dole's forehead, talking to him, trying to keep him there . . .

Dole could feel the rain on his head, legs wouldn't move in this mud, had to get by them all, get the pass, Bud can throw the ball long, Bud Smith can throw, had to get his arms up, Bud would see him, get behind, to the end zone, couldn't move in the mud, couldn't move his legs, couldn't make them go, like running through water, mud all over him, Mom'll have a fit, soaked all over, got to get home, she'll be there, get the mud off, dinner, be clean before dinner at the table, everybody's probably sitting already, at the table, Mom in the kitchen where were the others, where were they? Where were they?

After someone finally got the Kraut machine-gun bastards, McBryar left Dole in the ravine, climbed the knoll behind, trying to flag a medic. There was no one coming for them. *Jesus, we're gonna die out here.* Artillery was still coming in. Couldn't tell anymore whose it was. McBryar got hit. Hit, or knocked down. He got a concussion, they said. He was still woozy hours later, had just enough sense left to show 'em where Dole lay, in blurry dusk, when the medics found them, and packed them both off to the field hospital.

———

At the hospital, nine hours after he was hit, they figured he was going to die. Whatever hit him exploded inside, broke his collarbone and the shoulder behind it, not to mention his arm. Worst thing was, it smashed into his vertebrae, crushed a piece of his spine, it was broken, the spinal cord was knocked out. He couldn't move. He couldn't feel anything below his neck.

So they cleaned him up, splinted what they could reach, sent him down to the hospital in Pistoia, near Florence. But the only thing they could do there was cut him open wide, see if they could spot anything pressed against the spinal cord. Captain Woolsey was the surgeon, thought he might find out what the problem was. But when he opened Dole up, there wasn't much to go by: nothing was in the right place, and half of it wasn't there. They just sewed him up. Nothing more to do. If he lived, sure as hell, he was never going to walk. Of course, they didn't tell him that. Woolsey and the hospital chief, Colonel Prosser, told him he was going to be fine. He'd just have to give it time . . .

Dole's eyes searched their faces. His eyes were about all he could move. They had his right arm up in traction, and a sling under his chin, attached to weights over the back of his bed, to keep his head from moving. He stayed like that for weeks, with no feeling in his arms or legs, like the body on the bed belonged to someone else. There were a couple of guys from his company in the hospital, Oanes and Johnson, country boys, like him— Johnson was from Kansas. Both of them could walk, and they'd come to his bedside, try to adjust his pillows, try to tell him he'd be all right. At night, after the nurses came with his hypo, a syringe full of sedative to kill the pain, to make him sleep, Oanes and Johnson would take Bob's Army comb and comb his thick black hair to ease him, to help him go to sleep.

After a while, the doctors put him in a cast, from his chin down to his legs. They crated him for shipment like a piece of china, all but his left arm. They were going to send him out on a hospital ship. Told him they could probably do more for him outside the war zone. But he was still in Pistoia on May 2, when the Germans surrendered in Italy. The U.S. grunts had broken through, got by the hills and crossed the Po. Then the Eighty-fifth beat the Jerries back to the Brenner Pass, sealed it off, and the Germans folded. Moreover, the breakout in Italy had killed the Führer's last hope of reinforcing the Reich. In five days, Hitler would be dead in his Berlin bunker. The war in Europe was over . . . but too late for Dole. That night, they took the blackout paper off the hospital windows. He saw daylight the next day. But that was the only difference.

They were celebrating the news in Russell, how the shooting was over where Bobby Joe was, when the telegram came in to Western Union. It was funny, how the news came. The Western Union man, James Weilman, was Doran's neighbor. He used to bring the War Department wires for Doran to deliver. Doran was good at that kind of thing, a comfort, in that kind of time. Even the church used to call Doran, to go sit with someone. So this was the only wire of the war that Weilman had to deliver. He brought it over, and had to tell Doran, this one was for him.

The wire said "seriously wounded," but that wasn't what the doctors thought. The guy was finished—as far as movement was concerned, anyway. And sooner or later, that meant infection, or pneumonia, or a half-dozen other diseases that preyed on a bedridden man. The best they could do was ship him to the big hospital for the Med, the Seventieth General, in Casablanca. Maybe they could do something for him there. Maybe, if the bones healed, he'd get some feeling back in his limbs. Maybe. It was a surprise already, the way this guy hung on.

A few nights before they shipped him out, Captain Woolsey

was in the ward for his rounds, and he called Colonel Prosser over.

Woolsey said to Dole: "Lieutenant, show the Colonel what you can do."

For half a minute nothing happened.

"Go ahead, Lieutenant, show him."

And then, with great effort, with the muscles in his jaw twitching from the effort, Dole raised his left arm four inches off the sheet on his chest.

———

Hello, Mr. and Mrs. Dole:

I'm sure you know that Robert is unable to write so I tried to write him a note. He told me what to write. I know you are worrying about Robert but I wouldn't worry too much because there isn't any doubt in my mind at all but what he will be just as good a man when he gets well as he was before he was hurt.

Just thank God it wasn't any worse than it was. That's the way I feel about it. In case you want to know who I am, my name is John Booth of Bethany, Mo. Robert was my Platoon Leader. He is a fine fellow. I'll write again for him. (A sniper shot me in the foot. I can't walk very well but it won't be long until I can.)

As always,
John

———

They were going to ship him back to Kansas, to the Winter General Army Hospital, some Quonset huts in a camp near Topeka. There wasn't anything they could do there, but it was

policy: if they were going to die, they should die near home . . .
saved the shipping cost.

Bina was there when he got to Winter General on June 12,
1945. Bob had the nurses take his arm out and lay it on his cast,
so his mother could see it. She'd steeled herself, but the minute
she came into the room, Bina broke down in tears. When she
saw the way he looked at her, she told herself that was the last
time she'd cry in front of Bob. And she sat down next to him and
touched his face.

She had to pick eight cigarette butts out of his plaster cast.
She told her sisters: they'd used her boy for an ashtray on the
train.

———

Bina moved into an apartment across the street from the hospital. She was there every day, to take care of Bob. When she was
with him now, she was brave, but she'd sob on the phone to
Doran: he was like a baby again . . . she had to feed him with a
spoon, wipe the drip from his chin . . . Bina washed every bit of
him that was out of the cast. Bob was always so particular . . .
but the smell that came up from that cast! It was enough to
make you retch! The nurses who'd fed him for the last two
months had spilled bits of food down into the cast. It smelled
like something died in there. Maybe something did. Sometimes
she'd look at him and she had to run out of the room, to weep in
a corner of the hallway.

"Don't cry, Mom," Bob used to tell her. He tried to be brave
for her, too. "I'm gonna be back, good as before." That wasn't
exactly what the doctors said, but if it was a matter of will, he'd
make it. He knew what he had to do: get back on his feet, get his
strength back. Then, he was going back to school, to play for

Phog Allen. Maybe not this September, no, but he was going to play again.

As for the doctors, they talked about a long haul, chipping away bit by bit at the body cast, as feeling and movement came back to his legs, his left arm. As for the right arm, well, they didn't say much. Even at best, it was going to be months before he could start to relearn the basics: to control his bladder and bowels, to sit up, maybe turn himself over. And longer still for bigger things, like walking to a bathroom, or bringing food from a plate to his mouth. That's what preyed on him: he couldn't do anything. He lay there, day after day, one day like the last, marked, if he was lucky, by some medical event, another few inches off the cast, or a moment's success moving one leg, then the other, under his sheet.

In those moments of triumph, he was sure: he'd make it back; he was going to play again. Then there'd be days of failure, no progress, or worse, constant pain, a seizure, violent shaking when he tried to move. He itched. He felt dirty in his cast. He stunk. Then the bleakness would descend upon him, or the rage. Why him? *What the hell did I do so wrong?* What Bina saw, what broke her heart was, he was so ashamed. He was a boy who'd defined himself by the strength of his body, how he could run, how hard he could work, how much he could lift. When her sister Mildred came to visit, what struck her was the way Bob talked about himself, like a piece of garbage, a cake dropped on the floor. Mildred came in and saw him in the bed, on his back. The face looked like Bob, but the rest was plaster. She bent down and patted his chest, tried to kiss him. He cringed. She said, "I brought you a banana pie."

"Good," he said, but then he was silent.

She tried to smile. "Well, you listen to us jabber," she said, and she turned to Bina. Then, she heard his voice:

"Don't have anything to say, anyway."

After that, he asked his mother to keep everybody else away. Doran and Bob's sister Norma Jean drove the hundred and eighty miles east, every weekend. But Bina was there day after day. She'd always hated tobacco, but she sat by his head and held cigarettes to his mouth. A smoke was the only pleasure left to him. Sometimes she read to him, but she kept the papers away, in case there was news about Bud Smith. Bud was lost in the Pacific, listed officially "missing in action," but no one from Russell, Kansas, would be fooled by that. They knew they'd get the bad news on Bud.

Bob's KU housemate, Dick Finney, from Topeka, had also been shot down in the Pacific, and his mother used to stay with Bina at the hospital. Helping Bina with Bob took her mind off her own son. It was near the end of June when Mrs. Finney was called away to the hospital phone. Her husband was on the line: "We got a message from the War Department." Bina couldn't be much comfort to her friend. Bob had caught a fever, it wouldn't leave him . . . and the doctors had no idea what to do.

Bina sat helpless in the smell of the ward at Winter General, while the fever grew and took Bob away. All the progress, the tiny triumphs of movement, were lost. Finally, Bina called Doran in Russell: "You got to come down. I'm afraid he won't make it through the night." Doran and Norma Jean started racing east on Route 40. Police cars with sirens gave them an escort into Topeka. The Russell police had called ahead. When they got to the hospital, Bina was still in the room, but it didn't matter. Bob didn't know who was there anymore. The nurses kept a tongue catcher on Bob's tray in case he went into seizure. A chaplain was hanging around in the hall, to be there, "in case . . ."

Finally, the doctors decided it had to be his kidneys: he couldn't make water, even with a catheter. His right kidney was full of stones, infected. They could take out the kidney, but not with this fever. It was measured at 108.7 degrees. They'd have to wait, try to force it down with the miracle drug of the age, penicillin. It could cut the infection and fever in a few days—if he could hold on a few days . . .

———

Bob held on, and made it through the operation. The fever disappeared and the other kidney worked, and by fall, they'd chipped away the whole cast. Now they were trying to get him out of bed. They hung his legs over the edge of the mattress, but it made him weak with fatigue. It took days to get him on his legs, and then he shook so, with the pain and the strangeness, they had to set him back in bed.

When Bob would start to shake, Bina had to leave the room. But soon she'd be back smiling bravely again. Now only the right arm was in traction. Every day, they'd get him out of bed, and he could take a few steps before he got tired. He could still barely move, but the doctors said he could go home. There wasn't anything more they could do. So Doran drove east and took Bob back to Russell. The neighbors watched from their windows, while the Doles got their boy into the house on a stretcher. The biggest, strongest kid from Russell High now weighed 122 pounds.

Bina and Doran put Bob in their bedroom, the front room with the French doors that led to the living room. They slept in the back, the children's bedroom. They rented a hospital bed and a rolling tray. Bob liked to have those French doors open, while Bina rushed around, cooking and doing for him. Kenny was just back from the war, but more than ever, Bob came first. Bina would feed him, bathe him, dress him, comb his hair, hold his cigarette to his mouth, carry the bedpan back and forth, go to the bathroom with him. There weren't enough hours in the day for all she wanted to do for him. She'd wake up at dawn thinking about what he could wear that would be comfortable to lounge in, and what she could cook, what he'd like, what would make the day special. She worked herself to the frayed edge of exhaustion, though she would never let Bob see that. And when Bob got down, Bina would crumble. Sometimes, with her sisters or her daughters, safe in the kitchen, where Bob couldn't hear, Bina would cry like a baby. She'd stand at the kitchen sink sobbing. "I'm afraid we brought him home to die."

At night, Doran would sit with Bob, read to him from *The Salina Journal*. Or he'd have Chet Dawson and his wife, Ruth, over to play bridge late at night, after the drugstore closed, so Bob could listen through the open French doors to news of the town and the farmers. Chet would call in the afternoon, say: "Bina? What're you cookin'? . . . Well, save some for me. I'll be by sometime." Bob didn't mind the Dawsons, but he didn't want anyone else to see him. He was so ashamed of the way he looked. There'd be time enough for them to see, when he was whole again, when he could play. That was the dream that kept him going. He was going to play ball for Coach Allen. It was more than a dream. It was a plan. He'd count off months in his head, what he'd be able to do with his arms and legs two months from now, four months, six . . . how he'd start to run, build his endurance. . . . But then, when someone came, even a good friend, he'd see in their eyes: "Poor Bob!" Their eyes made him see himself as they did. . . . "Poor Bobby Joe!". . . . And then the plan was only a dream, a pipe dream.

Bina let him talk on about how he'd play ball . . . whatever he wanted. What was the point of telling him anything else? For her part, talk of the future was bright, and immediate.

How about his favorite, liver and onions, tomorrow?

Bob, will you wear your new sweater this Sunday?

Or Christmas! . . . Christmas was always a big deal in that house, and this year, it would have to be double-special. Doran always got the biggest tree. If it didn't touch the ceiling, it was no good. And by the time he finished, that tree was a work of art. He'd trim off the uneven branches, and wherever the tree was thin, he'd drill into the trunk and insert the branches that he'd trimmed off before. Then, when he'd hang the icicles, he wouldn't throw them on any which way. He'd start on the inside and work his way out in circles, every icicle just right or he wouldn't be satisfied. Of course, that's how Bina wanted it, too.

She'd wreath every doorway in the house with evergreens. And every table had to be covered with Christmas cookies. Not just the tables. The counters, the floor . . . cookies everywhere, and all made with butter and cream, and frosted by Bina herself. Bina did everything for Christmas herself . . . her own popcorn balls, with caramel coating, or red ones, or chocolate-covered. She'd make her own taffy, so the family could come for taffy pulls. And shopping! That year, when Bob came home, she was already shopping for Christmas in the summer. And she was going to Kansas City for special things. She had her list for Bob all ready in a drawer.

But by Thanksgiving, Bob was gone again. He went to a special Army hospital in Michigan, where they did modern miracles in orthopedics. It was Uncle Sam's special center for paraplegics and amputees. Why should he wait around for Christmas?

More movement, more feeling in his left arm! The strength

to walk on his own legs for ten minutes, twenty, an hour! To run! And a miracle for his right arm, to let him play ball. To be whole again. That's what he wanted for Christmas.

But there was no miracle for Bob. On the fourth day before Christmas, he woke with a savage pain in his chest. It was a blood clot in his lung, the price of lying immobile so long. The doctors in Michigan started treating him with dicumarol, a vicious drug to thin the blood. It turned him, temporarily, into a hemophiliac.

But there was no choice. If the blood clot loosened from the wall of his lung and went to his heart, he was a dead man. He was strictly confined to bed again. This time he demanded that doctors tell him the outlook, straight. And they told him, it was fifty-fifty he'd live.

So he stayed in bed for weeks, then months, while all his strength ebbed away. As the new year stretched into its second month, he was weaker and weaker, and now the fever was back. The doctors tried cutting off the dicumarol. But the pain returned, and chills . . . the fever was eating him away. So they started the drug again, with penicillin, but the antibiotic couldn't stop this infection. He was coughing and rattling in his bed. Pneumonia was filling his lungs.

Bina and Doran drove back and forth from Kansas to Michigan, but they could see that the doctors had no plan. They couldn't stop the fever, so they packed him in ice. They had Bobby Joe packed like a fish in the market! By the end of February, Bob grew worse and the hospital called again, but Bina couldn't bear to go back . . . when Bob didn't know her, when the fever had him. So Kenny went to Michigan. He figured he was going just to pick up the body. It wasn't even Bob in that bed. It was just a shell of him.

"Is there any hope?" Kenny asked. They told him about an experimental drug. The Army had the only supply, a thirty-day dose for three patients. Bob would be the third. Would Kenny authorize the treatment?

"Well, what happened to the others?"

One died and one went blind, but he lived.

"What are his chances without it?"

Without it, nothing.

So Kenny called home, and Bina and Doran came back to Battle Creek, to sign the form, to watch the treatment. They had Bob tied down in bed, so he'd be still while the new drug took hold. Doctors told them not to expect much. Even if it worked, there was no guarantee he'd know them, be able to move, get the strength back he had before. No one really knew what this drug would do. It was called streptomycin.

So, beginning of March, they put him on it. Four days later, he sat up in bed, asked Kenny to go downtown and get him a milkshake.

1947

He was knocked back to childhood, learning to walk, eat, dress himself, write . . . but without even a baby's physical attainments: control of limbs, the strength to reach, push, grab. And without a child's sense of wonder, without the fresh triumph of discovery. Instead, there was the knowledge of what was lost, how he used to run, pull, lift: the sense that Bob Dole was not whole anymore.

Percy Jones Army Medical Center was Uncle Sam's place for miracles, where amputees got new arms and legs, and new lives to go with them, a place where spinal paraplegics started moving, got up and walked again. It was opened after Pearl Harbor in a single massive building in Battle Creek, Michigan, an old-fashioned sanatorium endowed by the Kellogg cereal fortune, with a sweeping lawn and a grand central staircase in the echoing entry hall. By the time Dole checked in, Percy Jones was a small city in itself—with a population bigger than Russell, Kansas.

But with all the Army's assembled wizardry, there was no

orthopedic shortcut for Dole. His was a solitary battle, maddeningly slow. The nurses could lift him out of traction, help him off his bed, but after that, it was up to Bob how many baby steps he could take. One day, by act of will, he might walk to the end of the hall, and his hope for a miracle would swell again. He was going to make it back, whole, good as new—back at school, he'd play for Phog Allen. . . . But then, the next morning, in the whirlpool, a therapist might work for two hours, unsuccessfully, trying gently to pry two fingers apart on the claw of his right hand. Or Dole might lie in traction all day, trying, until sweat rolled down his face, to move two fingers together, on his left hand. And if he could not, the world went black, and there was Dole alone again, just his will—that was all he recognized of himself—trapped in a hospital bed with his nemesis, this body.

The doctors could ease the struggle sometimes: if he had pain, there was Demerol. But the narcotics knocked out his will, too, and that he could not let them take. That was all he had, and he learned to hide it, deep inside, where nothing could touch it; not the false cheer of doctors, nor even his own family's brave smiles; not the pain from his body, nor even the evidence of his reason, his own racing brain that told him, screamed in his head, the ugly fact that he would not hear, that he could not accept: he would *never* be what he was.

How could he ever let that worm bore to his center: What the hell would he do then? Play bridge all day, like the guys in the ward, with his cards held in a special rack, while someone else shuffled his turn? And after that, what would he do? Sell pencils on Main Street? Sometimes, he could actually *see* himself on Main Street, Russell, in a wheelchair, with a cup. That was his private vision of hell, the spur to get him up, trying again. He didn't tell anybody about it, wouldn't let them near that part of him that still burned bright. And he didn't want it dulled with the dirty facts of the here and now, the needles, the hot-wax treatments that never loosened his hand, the bedpan-bedsore-nuts-and-bolts of hospital life. So, whenever they came to talk, no matter who they were, or how well intentioned, there was always a joke to hold them off, something about the weather, or a nurse, or another guy on the ward. The doctors and nurses marveled at him: that Lieutenant Dole was just *wonderful*, so full of good humor. They started to wheel him around to other wards. He'd cheer up the rest of the fellows.

But what about him? Where was his cheer? It got to be frighteningly clear to Dole, the Army had no miracle for him— not at Percy Jones. After months there, he could barely walk, there was still no movement in his right arm, almost no feeling in his left hand. And there was no plan to do much about it— not that he could divine. So he got leave to go home to Russell. If he had to make his miracle himself, he'd do it. If the doctors in Michigan couldn't straighten out his arm, he'd do it alone. So Kenny came back to Michigan and brought Bob home on the train. Bina and Doran moved once again to the children's bedroom, in the back of the house. Once again, they rented a hospital bed and a rolling tray for the front room. Doran, Kenny, and some neighborhood fellows hooked up ropes and pulley-weights from old sash windows on the wall of the garage, behind the house, so Bob could work on his strength, every day.

And Bob worked, alone, day and night, on his problem. That's what he called it, his problem: there were no good words for this enemy, his body. What words could anybody use that would not burrow into him and eat at the will that was keeping him alive? It wasn't that he chose to wall himself away, but what else could he do, when he heard those words that would never leave him? One day, when he was with Doran at the grain elevator, a farmer came in and, by way of chat, asked: "This your crippled son?" There wasn't a thing for Bob to say, but for days after, he was clouded over with gloom and rage. One afternoon, when he'd been home awhile, he screwed up his courage and walked to Dawson Drug. Main Street seemed a hundred miles long. He was sure everybody was looking at him—120 pounds: he was a spectacle!—the way his feet shuffled, his right arm cocked up in a lead brace that a high school pal, Adolph Reisig, made for him at his auto body shop. Bob got into the drugstore and hauled himself, without help, onto a seat at the counter. But even then his bones wouldn't sit right on the stool. Bub and Chet had to adjust him for balance, like a rickety piece of furniture. One of the geezers at the wooden-top tables said: "Gee, that's too bad. . . . You prob'ly wished they woulda finished you off . . ." Bob turned and glared, felt his face flush hot. "If I thought like that, I'da been dead a long time ago." But for months, he didn't go back to Dawson's.

He worked alone. He pulled down the dark curtain of reserve that he could not lift again, even when he chose. He'd spend all day behind the house, working himself to exhaustion with the ropes on the garage wall. Bina would stand at the back door and call: "Bob, don't you want to rest? Bob! Come in and rest awhile . . ." He'd just say: "No." He'd growl it. Or he wouldn't answer. He'd pull harder. He was trying to pull with the bad right arm. If he could straighten that out, he'd play again. Even when he was in the house, he'd be squeezing a rubber ball, or a nutcracker, with the left hand. Even when he sat in a chair, his legs were moving. Time was weighing on him:

months were flying by, and he felt he was standing still. He could walk around the block, but that wasn't good enough. He pushed it, faster, harder, until he was dragging his bony form along in a shuffling run. He brought the lead arm brace back to Adolph in the body shop: he wanted more lead in it, more, and more, a constant weight, so it ached, so he knew he was working it every minute.

There was no schedule in the house anymore, except for Bob's racing internal clock. Chet and Ruth Dawson would show up to play bridge at midnight, and Bina'd do a load of wash while the card game went on around her. Food was whatever he wanted, when he wanted, and where: if Bob said he'd like to be outside, Bina would move the whole show outdoors: tablecloth, silver, the dishes with the pattern of pink blossoms and green leaves. . . . Or Bina'd ask Bob in the middle of the morning: "You want a Coke?" And everyone would pile into the car, and ride out to the highway. Norma Jean would come in the afternoons, and Bob would ask: "You doin' anything tonight? . . . No?" And then she'd stay with him in the front room and rub that arm for hours. Gloria was married by then, living out of town, but she'd come back to visit, too, mostly to talk to Bob. She'd ask about the war sometimes, in case he wanted to get it off his chest. But Bob would only say, "Agh, the heroes are still over there." He meant the dead ones. That put an end to the questions. Now Kenny was married, too, living with his beautiful Dottie in a little brick house, right next door. Of course, Kenny was still on call. If Bob had to go anywhere, Kenny took him. (He was driving Bob back to Michigan on Dottie's twenty-first birthday.) But mostly, it was Bina who did for Bob. Kenny would do for Bina. And she wasn't shy about asking. More and more, as Bob's problem wore her down, she didn't have patience for anyone else. When Dottie was in labor with Kenny's first child, Bina visited her in the delivery room and rasped: "Are you all right?"

Dottie said: "Feel like I'm gonna die."

"Aw, you'll live," Bina snapped, and went back home to Bob.

On his darker days, Kenny's marriage and his new baby girl were hard for Bob, too. It wasn't that he grudged it to his younger brother—not at all. But Bob was the elder . . . always a mile out in front of that kid. And now Kenny was a husband, a father . . . and Bob? Treading water, trying to get back to where he was. Who would *he* live his life with? Who'd take him now . . . like this? Did he even have the right to impose his . . . problem? No, he'd probably be alone. Hell, he was alone. No matter how everybody did for him, how long they sat and talked with him, how late they stayed up to see if they could get him to sleep . . . when it got down to it, it was Bob, alone. Sometimes, Dottie would wake, next door, to give the baby a bottle or quiet her in her crib. And through the darkness outside, she'd hear the music from Bina's house. It was Bob, with the record player he got when he went off to KU. And he'd play that song, over and over, Jane Froman's song from *Carousel* . . .

> *When you walk through a storm,*
> *hold your head up high*

Sometimes, after he played that song, you could see he felt better, and he'd say, "How 'bout s'more music?" And he'd play it again, and whistle along.

Walk on, walk on
with hope in your heart,
And you'll never walk alone.
You'll never walk alone!

And then, everyone was lighter. Even Bina was happy. But just as suddenly, the dark curtain could descend. One day, back by the garage, Bob fell and couldn't get up. "Never gonna work . . ." he was muttering afterward. "Terrible . . . crawling around like an *animal*." Then there was *nothing* they could do for him. That was the awful fact at the bottom of their every day. It didn't matter what they did for him. It didn't *count* unless he could do it himself. He *had* to do it alone. Now he wouldn't let anyone light a cigarette for him. Sometimes, with a match, he'd char his numb left hand black . . . but don't try to get in his way. Or, he'd be sitting at the table, getting along okay with a fork in that balky left hand. But then a piece of food would tumble to his lap. And his face would go dark with helpless rage. And he wouldn't say a word. He'd just get up and walk out. No one dared follow him, or say anything.

One afternoon, the family came home, and there was no Bob—not in the bedroom, the living room, he wasn't out back, pulling on the ropes. Bina called Dawson's, then Doran: no Bob, not a sign of him. Finally, they looked inside the garage, and there he was, hanging from the rafters by the bad right arm. Hanging with his feet swinging off the floor. Soaked and trembling with sweat and pain. Bina burst into tears right there. Thought he was dead. But his will was alive: Bob wouldn't come down. If he could straighten out that arm, he was going to play ball again.

He was still hunting the miracle, when an uncle who'd served in the Medical Corps told him about Dr. K. This was Hampar Kelikian, who'd escaped to America as a boy, with twenty dollars and a carpet from his family home in Armenia, and had worked his way to eminence as a neurosurgeon in Chicago. Dr. K. knew about wars: his three sisters were killed in the massacres that posed as war in his native land; his brother, a soldier in World War II, was killed in the Italian campaign. Dr. K. also enlisted, in the Army Medical Corps: he became a pioneer in the restoration of damaged limbs. President Truman awarded him a medal for special contributions to military medicine. In 1947, Dole made his pilgrimage to Chicago.

Kelikian was a small man, with curly hair, prematurely gray. He was friendly, brisk, optimistic. He spoke with an accent, but no hesitation. He knew what could be done for Dole, and he knew he could do it. But he wanted Dole to know something, too: there wasn't going to be a miracle. He could give Dole partial use of the arm, maybe forty percent: the rest was up to Bob. He could jerry-rig a shoulder of sorts, but there was no way it would rotate: the arm would not lift; Dole would not play ball. What Dr. K. could do was corporeal carpentry, not magic. . . . That was the most important work he did for Dole, and he did it with words. There was something about Kelikian, his certainty, his self-possession, the big office in Chicago, or the way he'd pulled himself up by his own will . . . or maybe Dole was just ready. But he listened. Kelikian told him: "Don't think anymore about what you've lost. You have to think about what you have . . . and what you can do with it."

Kelikian would not take a fee for his work, not from Bob, not a dime. He'd do it out of gratitude to his adopted land. To Dr. K., Bob Dole represented something fundamental about the country: "This young man . . . ," the doctor said later. "He had the faith to endure."

Still, Dole would have to come back to Chicago, to check into a hospital, and this wasn't on the Army's ticket anymore. Back in Russell, Chet Dawson spread the news: Bob had to go to Chicago for an operation. And he put a cigar box on the drugstore counter: the Bob Dole Fund . . . the Dawson boys started it off with a few bills themselves. And Chet was post commander at the time, so the VFW took up the charge. Pretty soon, Bub Shaffer at the Home State Bank was taking collections, too. Then, they started across the street at the Russell State Bank, and then Banker's Mercantile and the rest of the shops pitched in. Everybody in town lent a hand, one way or another. One lady put thirty cents in the box—that was all she could afford. But there was some serious money, too, and by June, when Bina packed the car for the trip to Chicago, the people of Russell had collected one thousand eight hundred dollars to help Bob Dole get back on his feet.

It turned out there were three operations: the first to cut away the bone in the shattered shoulder, to hang the arm instead by a strip of muscle that Dr. Kelikian took from Dole's thigh. But in recuperation at Percy Jones, the arm wouldn't come down: it fused instead in front of Dole's chest, about at the level of his chin. So Kelikian went at it again, and after the second operation, the arm healed at Dole's side. It was as Dr. K. had told him: no miracle, nothing magic about it. The arm would hang shorter than his left arm, Dole would never be able to lift it much, or control it at full rotation. But the point was, Dole could do something with it. He could hold it a certain way—like this . . . and it looked like an arm again.

In a third operation, Kelikian tried to transplant muscle and tendon back to the right hand. Most of that didn't take, so Dole's fingers would always splay unnaturally on that right hand; but he learned he could roll it around a pen, a folded paper, something to give it shape. It started to look like a hand again.

The point was, he could do something with it. The biggest change was how Dole looked at it. Look what he could do! In October, Norma Jean was married, and Bob went to the wedding as best man. He wore his lieutenant's uniform—not the fussy dress stuff, but the Eisenhower jacket, with the square padded shoulders. He was thin, but his *eyes* . . . he looked so handsome. The minister put Norma Jean's ring onto one of Bob's fingers: that was the only way Bob could hold it, until the proper moment; but nobody saw that, the way Bob did it. What they saw was the way he stood up at Trinity Methodist, on Main Street, in front of all the guests, like a soldier, proud, straight as a rod.

Phyllis

Phyllis saw him first in March, across the mess hall at Percy Jones. He was still thin, had his arm in a splint, but what she noticed was his sharp dark eyes, his high brow and thick shining hair, the strong bones in his face. Phyllis said to her friend: "Who's *that?*"

"Oh, that poor Bob Dole. He doesn't have long to live, you know."

"Isn't that sad . . . such a nice-looking man."

Of course, her friend was behind the times: Bob Dole was going to live, and he was going to do something with that life. He was back at Percy Jones after Dr. K.'s operations, but he knew now it was just a way station.

He wasn't waiting anymore for a miracle. The hospital still gave him curare treatments for tremors, and therapy in the whirlpool every day, but he was working on himself in every way. He'd found himself sort of a job, selling Oldsmobiles modified for wounded war vets. He sold a couple at Percy Jones, and in the bargain, got himself a blue sedan with a left-hand gearshift. It wasn't long till the Army put a stop to such business. But that didn't mean Dole had to give up, to lie around in bed, or play bridge all day.

He and a couple of buddies were tearing through the books in the hospital library: there wasn't anything Bob Dole didn't want to know. At night, they'd sit up talking books, until the nurses called lights out . . . at which point, they'd sneak off the ward, and steal across the street, to a coffee shop that stayed open till two. Bob was thinking about getting out of the Army, going back to school, getting a degree. He'd talked to Kelikian about it. Maybe he could be a lawyer. "Why not?" said Dr. K.

It was March 12 when Bob showed up at the Officers' Club dance. Phyllis and her friends had done the decoration: it was Heaven and Hell—Hell, with the pictures of devils in flames, was the bar; it was in Heaven, the dance floor, under painted clouds and angels, where Bob spotted Phyllis, sitting with a group of nurses at a table. He stood straight and tall—no splint—in his uniform, as he walked up and asked her to dance.

"I'd love to," she said.

He couldn't put his right arm around her back—not by himself. But he put it on her hip, and Phyllis stepped right in. Years later, in Russell, she'd advise their women friends: "Dance close to Bob . . ." They always thought she was making a joke.

———

Phyllis Holden wasn't the kind to make jokes—not about things that mattered. She'd grown up in rural New Hampshire, a girl so tenderhearted she never could stand teasing. Sometimes, like every well-loved child, she'd do something so cute that her parents laughed with joy. But Phyllis thought they were laughing at

her, and she'd start to cry. As she came of age, there was a soft-
ness about her that drew a flock of young men. But until she got
to Percy Jones, she was not lucky in love.

At the University of New Hampshire, in the new program
for occupational therapy, she'd got engaged to a fellow named
Joseph Bennett, who was badly infected with malaria from his
days on Guadalcanal. That engagement lasted almost three
years, but in the end, it fell apart. After college, in her resident
training, she got involved with a young man who had os-
teomyelitis. That never got beyond a "serious friendship," but
her parents were horrified. "My God, Phyllis," her mother
scolded. "Why don't you get away from these lame ducks!"

But she loved the work. It was a new field, exciting, and
Phyllis felt like a pioneer. She worked in the psychiatric wards,
teaching crafts, silver and leather. She was never scared of the
men. She thought even a schizophrenic would maintain some
respect for a woman. And the alcoholics would protect her, if
need be. Meanwhile, she was helping, she was needed, she was
good at her job. In '48, she decided to follow her college friend,
Elsie Deming, to Michigan, to the Army Medical Center, where
the big job was being done. She and Elsie would join the Army,
they'd see the world: Phyllis had never been west of New York
State. Anyway, there was not, at the moment, a love in her life
to keep her in New Hampshire. When Elsie met her at the station in Battle Creek, Phyllis laughed and said, "Tell you one
thing: the next time I get engaged, I'm going to get *married.* Just
give me time to get out the invitations . . ."

She almost didn't have time. Two days after she danced
with Bob Dole, he called—nine-thirty at night!—and asked her
out for a coffee. If it'd been anyone but that nice Lieutenant
Dole, she wouldn't have gone: he'd think she was sitting alone

by the phone. But everybody knew Bob was a nice guy, always had a good word for everyone, had a job selling cars . . . he didn't try to flirt with the nurses, like some of the men. So, she said yes. And he told her about Russell, Kansas, and his father in the grain elevator, his brother and two sisters, and Dr. Kelikian in Chicago, and the operations. . . . Then it was the Easter dance at the Officers' Club, and more coffee dates, always at night. She had her work and he had his therapy, so it wasn't like they spent every minute together. And Phyllis wasn't looking for anyone special. . . . But Bob was always fun, always so gracious, always opened the door of the Oldsmobile for her, always did the driving, always wanted to know about *her*, how *she* was doing. And he was brave about himself, and handsome, and smart. It was only a few weeks before she felt she wasn't interested in a date with anyone else. Then Bob had to go to Chicago, to see Dr. K., and Phyllis went with him. Kelikian was urging Bob to go to school. He smiled at Phyllis, and said: "She can go with you and take notes."

———

In April, Bob went back to Russell for a visit, and Bina got on the phone with her sister, right away. "I think Bob's fallen madly in love with a therapist."

"*Really?* How do you know?"

"That's eighty percent of his conversation! What a difference!"

Bob was like a kid again. He'd get up in the morning, jump into his car, and drive right down Main Street. Visit with Doran and the farmers in the elevator. Stop in at Dawson's, stay two hours! On and off the stools, over to the jukebox . . . "Heyy, how 'bout some music? . . ." Then back home, next door, to Kenny and Dottie. Told Dottie about the beautiful things Phyllis made with her hands. Phyllis can do this, Phyllis can do that. She's got long dark hair, dark eyes, real pretty, real slender. . . .

He told one friend: "Boy, she's filled in all the right spaces!"

Bina was teary with joy on the phone. "Lord, what a difference!"

———————

A month after the dance, Phyllis got the test results for her Army enlistment. She had allergies the Army was concerned about. "Well," Bob said, "you could prob'ly get out . . . if you got married . . ." Phyllis didn't speak. Bob said: "Aghh, think you could live in Russell, Kansas?" She said she thought she could, with Bob.

She called her mother on April 27, her birthday, and said she was getting married. "He's been paralyzed, but he's had a wonderful return. He's still got some paralysis in his right arm, but it doesn't seem to bother him . . ." Her mother hit the roof.

"Phyllis, you *can't* have another lame duck!"

"Oh, Mother!"

"My God, Phyllis! *You* said he can't button a button, zip a zipper! How's he ever going to earn a living?"

"He's going to go to college!"

"Well," Estelle Holden insisted, "your father and I think it's just too soon."

Within days, Estelle got a letter from Bob, analyzing his time in courtship with Phyllis. The way he figured, if it had been normal dating, say once or twice a week, it would have worked out to three years!

Estelle wrote back with her real reservations: "Phyllis is a very precious child to us, and we want the best for her. And unless you are capable of becoming a husband to her, in all ways, we don't think it would be a good idea."

That was hard for Bob to take. But Phyllis wouldn't let him get down about it. "Bob, it's just because they haven't met you."

She told her mother: *Make the announcement!* And she and Bob started driving east, to New Hampshire.

Two weeks later, Bina and Doran arrived, and Bob and Phyllis were married, June 12, 1948.

———

Kansas was land like Phyllis had never seen—no trees for miles, no hills or rocks like her home ground—but it was beautiful to her, at the end of that June. Phyllis was in love, and the harvest was on, the milo and beans were like rich green carpet, the ground checkered in emerald, gold, and deep brown, as Bob raced the Oldsmobile west on Highway 40, and told her about Russell. Bob said the earth there was *so flat* . . . on a good day, you could see Kansas City. Well, it wasn't quite like that. Kansas City was two hundred miles away.

But she would have believed him, if he'd insisted. She was so willing to see it as his eyes did. If this was to be her adopted home, then she'd embrace it, too. But in Russell, it wasn't quite that easy. For one thing, she came to make a home in a nest of ferocious homemakers. Actually, Phyllis knew how to cook—or thought she did: she'd even won a prize for a cake at the state fair in New Hampshire. But that wasn't cooking in Russell, heck no. She couldn't make the fried chicken like Bina (who could?), or the brownies, or the ice cream, or . . . the problem was, Bina's house was perfect, from the flowers bordering the lawn, to the shrubs and roses, the shiny scrubbed porch, and inside, the smell of flowers and wax, and the pie cooling on the dining room table, and not one dish out of place, unwashed, and the big embroidered white feedsack towels, the pink-and-green curtains on the French doors in the living room. It wasn't that Bina was mean about it, no . . . but you could see she noticed when something wasn't just so, and Bob must have noticed, too. Of course, he didn't say anything.

But Phyllis felt she had to be perfect for him—it was *expected*. She'd stand next to Bina for hours in the kitchen, watching and measuring what went into the bowl—Bina never had recipes. When Bob went to buy clothes, the tailor at Banker's was going to take in the shoulder of the suit, but Phyllis figured out how to pad it underneath, just so, and it looked perfect. . . . Then there was the matter of his neckties—she tied them. But she couldn't get the Windsor knot, with the dimple just so, and the front just a hair longer than the back, like Bob liked it. And this went on for *years*, and she asked their men friends, and the salesmen at Banker's to show her . . . but it still wasn't right. And, of course, she could see he noticed, they all did. . . . They were always watching Bob, jumping up to help him, getting something for him, or fixing something near him that wasn't quite right. . . .

That was the heart of the problem, how they treated Bob, too tenderly, like a thousand-year-old vase. It just reinforced his feeling that something wasn't right, wasn't whole, about him. One day that summer, in lawn chairs out in Bina's backyard, a glass of iced tea slipped from Bob's numb left hand and spilled at his feet. "Oh, God," Phyllis said, "can't you hold on to *anything?*" Bina and Kenny looked at Phyllis like she'd just spat on the Bible. How could she talk to Bob that way?

But, of course, that was the right way. That's one of the

things Bob loved about Phyllis: she never treated him like a cripple, an invalid . . . God, how he hated that word. . . . She'd tell him flat out not to wait to be waited on: "Do it yourself . . . you can do it!" She'd get after *him* to work on his body. "You've got that leg exercise to do . . . why don't you get that out of the way?" And she was so matter-of-fact, so sure of him and what he could do. "Pick up your feet, Bob. There's no reason to shuffle like that!" In time, Bina and the rest realized it was good for Bob. In Phyllis's eyes, he saw himself whole. And why not? She never saw him any other way.

Around town, where the citizens looked at Bob like their own prize experiment (they were the ones who put him back on his feet!), there was a myth already spreading on Phyllis, that she was Bob's therapist at the big Army hospital. Or, better yet, his nurse. She was the gal who nursed him back to life . . . and fell in love. . . . And no matter how many times Bob explained, or how many times Phyllis protested that Bob was well and strong again before she ever met him . . . well, people believe what they want to believe. Even years later, when he'd risen so high, no one wanted to believe her when she said that he was always the strong one . . . but she knew.

That September, they packed up the Oldsmobile again and started south, to Arizona, where Bob would go back to college, as a junior. The doctors recommended a hot-weather climate, after all the blood thinners Bob had taken. Of course, Bob drove all the way, and Bob found their two-room house . . . and although Phyllis did take notes (and wrote test papers from his dictation), it was Bob who did the work, who studied all night, each night, by memory, pacing their living room, barking German verbs in his prairie voice, over and over, until he had them in his head, until Phyllis finally had to ask: Bob, why? . . .

"Why do you have to get an A? Isn't a C good enough?"

And Bob snapped: "*You* tell me how to study a C's worth, and *I'll do it.* All I know's how to work till I get it."

He taught her how to play cribbage, but he didn't play, he had work to do. No one was going to have to cut Bob Dole any slack. There was a couple nearby who became good friends, and they'd go swimming, but Bob wouldn't undress. He didn't want anyone to see his problem. She could cut up his food for him at home, but not at a restaurant. He'd have them cut it in the kitchen and bring it out that way. He meant to be strong, and she relied on that, too.

One night, that autumn, when they were at dinner, Bob suddenly lurched in his chair, slumped over his plate and gasped: "Omigod . . . s'get to the VA . . . on the double."

Phyllis was scared to death. She was twenty-three, had never stayed a night alone. She'd never even driven in Tucson by herself. And now Bob was in the hospital. . . . It turned out he had another blood clot, but thinners took care of it. He was fine, in a week. Yet what she remembered was her shock, the way he looked at that moment, so frail! . . . It had never occurred to her that Bob could get sick.

1 9 5 2

The county election was the first chance folks had to get a good look at Bob. Of course, people knew him from Dawson Drug. But that was before. . . . And the farmers who knew Doran from the grain elevator, they'd heard about Bobby Joe. In fact, one way or the other, almost everybody had heard the story of that poor Dole boy, or if they hadn't, someone would whisper it ("carried 'im home on a stretcher, couldn't even feed himself . . . ") as they watched him around town, campaigning for County Attorney.

It wasn't much of a job, when you got down to it. You had all the criminal prosecution, all the county's civil legal business, and then, if you had time, you could take on private clients. You pretty much had to take outside work; the county job only paid $242 a month. The courthouse janitor made $10 more. (In the old days, there was always something extra from the bootleggers, but Kansas had gone wet in 1948, so that put an end to a source of steady income.) There were only a half-dozen lawyers in Russell, and the county job usually went to the last one, the youngest, who was trying to build a practice.

That was the problem in '52: there were two good boys come back to town, after the Army, law school, and all. And people said it was a darned shame there wasn't a pair of jobs. Dean Ostrum, Bob's opponent, was a boy of excellent family, too. He was Oscar's son; Oscar Ostrum was probably the best lawyer in Russell. And Dean was always smart: a debater at Russell High, where he likely did even better than Bob Dole; everybody knew Bob as an athlete, but Dean was the brainy sort. People naturally thought of Dean in the law—in that county job, matter of fact . . . till Bob announced.

Actually, he didn't so much announce it as murmur. . . . There was a political meeting in June, at the high school in Bunker Hill, a tiny town nine miles from Russell. Ray Shaffer was the Republican boss in Russell County, and he introduced Bob to the crowd. Bob stood with his arm hanging down, crooked at the elbow, his body canted a bit to the left, so he could try to hide "his problem," and he said to the crowd, in a single sentence, that he wanted the County Attorney job. Said it so fast and low, it didn't really sink in—people just stared— until he stopped, and sat down again. That was all the announcement he made. Next day, he got a new blue suit, on credit, at Banker's Mercantile—Phyllis taught the tailor how to put in the special shoulder pads—and Bob started passing out flyers on Main Street.

That was about as sophisticated as things got in that race. Oh, Bob had his brother, Kenny, and his friend, Adolph Reisig, and maybe a couple of the Krug boys—they called themselves the "tack and hammer men"—who'd nail up posters to get Bob's name in front of people's eyes. And maybe at the end, each candidate would drop twenty-five dollars for ten spots on the radio for Election Day. But mostly, this was one-on-one campaigning: Bob and Dean Ostrum, dogging one another's steps up Main Street, Russell, and then out to Bunker Hill, Gorham, Lucas, Luray, Fairport, Dorrance, Waldo, Paradise. . . . At least, Bob Dole made all those stops. Heck, if he was driving back from some one-street prairie town, and he spotted a light off in the endless fields, he'd dirt-road up to that house in the night, and let the dogs yowl until a light came on behind the screen door, so Bob could say: name is Dole, and he just stopped by to let them know—name's Bob Dole—he hoped, he'd be grateful—Dole, like the pineapple juice—to have their support on Election Day.

In theory, Bob was already a practicing attorney in Russell. He got a used desk and a brand-new hundred-dollar leather chair, and set them up in Doc Smith's office on Main Street. But really, what he was doing, from the time he got out of law school in June, was running flat out for that county job. By happenstance (and the boom in oil, sparked by the war), that was the year Russell peaked in population—maybe seventy-five hundred people in town, another five thousand spread out around the county. Still, there couldn't have been any more than five thousand voters, and Bob probably asked for every one of those votes, personally.

In theory, he was already a veteran of public office, having been installed for a single term in the lower house of the Kansas State Legislature, while he was in Topeka, at Washburn University Law School. But that wasn't anything like this. The legislature only met for three months during his two-year term—it wasn't a job for a grown man, not full-time—and Bob (or, to be precise, his Republican backers in Russell County) had the powerful argument that Bob was already there, in Topeka, and at least the voters wouldn't pay for gasoline, back and forth. As for Bob, he held that post in his spare time—didn't even break stride in school. Barely mentioned to Phyllis that he was going into politics: she wasn't that interested; and what the heck, he'd be home every night, same as always.

In theory, Bob was already fully recovered from his injuries. That was the party line, anyway. He was still thin, of course, and he had that arm—everybody could see that, no matter what he did. But you wouldn't think of him as still healing, not by seeing him on the street, or talking to him, watching him work. Bob made sure of that. In fact, this was the recovery: showing himself, and his nemesis, his body, in every corner of the county, to any voter who'd stop and chat. That, and winning . . . that would be the ultimate recovery: to have those thousands of his home folks—everybody who knew him, really—ratify with their ballots that he was a man who could work for them. For that he'd keep going, till his was the last light you could see on Main Street. And he'd be up and at it by seven the next morning, as soon as Phyllis finished tying his tie. . . .

He wasn't afraid of work—only of no work. It wasn't so long since he'd starred in his own private nightmare, the vision of Bob Dole in his wheelchair, selling pencils on Main Street. What he feared were the silent flashes of that vision in other people's eyes—he searched their faces when he asked for a vote: Did they think he wasn't up to a "real" job? In fact, a lot of people thought this might be just the way to get Bob into a job "he could handle." But nobody said that to Bob. There was something in the way he carried himself that warned off sympathy—would have broken his heart.

Of course, there were also some codgers who just didn't

care. One old farmer greeted Bob at the door and told him he knew his granddad . . .

"Agh, good," Bob said.

"Used to butcher for me . . ."

"Yeah, he was a pretty good butcher . . ."

"No he wasn't," the farmer said. "Gave me bad sausage. Never liked him."

Back in town, Bob would tell that story with relish. He'd tell it with an air of droll complaint—can you *believe* some people? It was funny, but it showed—he hoped it showed—that no one was cutting a break for Bob. No, sir. Bob was never afraid of what people would say—only of what they wouldn't say.

And he never forgot anything people said, the way they looked, their kinfolk he knew . . . kept it all in his head. If someone mentioned they'd be at their church Sunday after next for their parents' anniversary—everyone in the family's coming by for ice cream and cake . . . well, they learned after a while, they'd see Bob that Sunday, too. He wouldn't make a show of it: just stopped by to say hello . . . but the people were so surprised he showed up, they'd always make a point of introducing "their special guest." Then, of course, they'd want to feed him ice cream and cake, but he wasn't going to try to work a fork with his left hand in front of everyone, so he wouldn't be able to stay, and they'd wrap up a couple of pieces for him, which, of course, he'd remember when he saw them again, and mention how good that cake was, how he'd like to get the recipe for Phyllis . . .

There didn't seem to be any limit to what he could keep in his head. Nobody much remarked on it: they all thought he just remembered *them*. The only one who really knew was Phyllis, but it was old hat to her. That's the way she'd seen him go after law school, night after night, in their tiny apartment (in a building named The Senate) in Topeka. In his first year back at college, Phyllis had gone with Bob to take notes, in a few of his classes, but after that, the VA gave him a machine, one of the first recording machines manufactured. It was called a Sound-Scriber, a big, clunky brown box with a black microphone-mouthpiece and a heavy needle arm that grooved a recording into green plastic disks, like little record albums. Bob would carry that machine into class and set it up on the arm of a chair, up in front, where the professor's words would be clearest. At night—sometimes all night—he'd sit at home (while Phyllis tried to keep quiet), playing those scratchy green disks, over and over, noting a couple of words in his painstaking left-hand squiggles, then putting the pen down, lifting the needle, and carefully setting it back on the disk to get the next few words. In those days, the law was practiced without dictating machines, and that box in the classroom spooked some people—even professors. Bob had to get official permission to use it, after one student complained that those disks gave Dole an advantage. But it never felt that way to Bob. He never could take many notes. Mostly, what he could do was hear that voice, on the disks, over and over, until he could say it in his head, until he knew that case, with all the citations—until he could literally dictate that learning back to Phyllis, who would write his exam.

Sometimes, he'd study with his friend Sam Crow—of course, Sam had notes. He even offered to copy them for Bob. But that wouldn't do Bob any good. He had to have it in his head. That old apartment building, The Senate, had louvered doors out to the hallways, to let the air circulate, and when the weather was warm, you could hear a whole lesson on contracts or torts, in the hall, before you even got to Bob's door. Then, inside, at a little desk, just to the right of the door, there he'd be, sallow and skinny in his T-shirt, which hung uneven on his neck, sloped down on one side, where there was no shoulder: that was the side Bob kept his pack of Camels rolled up in the sleeve. Sam and his wife, Ruth, would come over in the evenings, and the girls would take turns treating each other to the movies, while Sam and Bob went at the cases—Sam had his notes, Bob had his head. When the girls came back, they might stop for coffee, after which Sam and Ruth would head home, and Phyllis to bed. She would still hear Bob on his cases, as she dropped off to sleep.

Bob never talked to Sam or Ruth about his injury, about the war. He was still painfully shy—considered himself a ruin. But he knew he'd have to get over that. Even then he was thinking politics, as a career. So Sam and Bob enrolled in a night class at the local high school—Beginner's Speech. For Bob, it was the moral equivalent of fire-walking: a test every time he showed up. In one of the first lessons, the teacher asked: "If you saw someone you knew walking down the street, would you cross the street to avoid him?"

Bob answered, "Sure."

But in class, he couldn't avoid showing himself. He had to get up on the raised stage, stand up tall, and talk, while the eyes of the rest were upon him. The little podium, at center stage, wouldn't hide his arm, no matter how he shifted. . . . "Bob!" the teacher would prod. "Why don't you say what you want to say, instead of shuffling around, and making us all wonder?"

After a while, speech class was like law school—sure, it was hard. But Bob had to be good. No matter what he had to do, no matter what he feared . . . nothing compared to the fear that people would pity him, expect from him any less than the rest, figure they had to cut slack for Bob Dole. It was never going to happen. Getting by was just not enough. He had to graduate from law school with distinction. He had to stand up in speech class and get his point across.

And now, he had a point to make, all over Russell County. He wanted that County Attorney job. He needed it. It didn't matter what he had to do. So anytime Bob could buttonhole a voter, better yet, a dozen, he'd stand up and say what he meant to say:

"Well, I didn't grow up with all the advantages," Bob would begin. "Had to work . . ." And he could almost see heads start to nod, as he bore into it. He never had to mention Dean Ostrum's name. People could fill in the blanks: son of a prominent attorney, had a car to drive to school, didn't play football— probably tennis was more in his line . . . the message was clear enough. Dean Ostrum didn't need that job, not like Bob. Bob Dole came from the world of work, weather, and want, like the farmers who would vote him into office. . . . Dean Ostrum would find a job, and if he didn't, he'd never go hungry. Bob wanted those farmers to know who was their kind, who would understand them, who grew up with Kansas dirt under his nails . . . like theirs. It got so tough out there for Dean, he started wearing frayed shirt collars, just to show he had some. But the people knew who Oscar Ostrum was, just as they knew Doran Dole.

Funny thing about it, Dean knew, too: from the day it came down to him and Bob, Dean figured he was going to lose. Bob Dole would just out-need him, and outwork him, run him into the ground. Dean kept at it, but after a while, it was like the steam just came out of him. Dean knew in his heart, it didn't matter what he did. . . .

"How long was my day?" Dean said, later, when it was just

a wistful memory. "I don't know, but it wasn't as long as Bob Dole's. I'm sure of that."

When the votes came in, it was Dole 1,133, Ostrum 948. And Bob Dole was in politics.

———————

People said there never was a County Attorney like Bob Dole. It was probably because he had a question in his own mind—could he do it?—that he worked so hard. There never was a time when he wasn't working, seemed like. He'd get to the courthouse, his second-floor office, maybe eight, eight-thirty. Usually, he'd have court in the morning, if the judge was in Russell that day. It wasn't that crime was such a problem—crime like we know it, anyway—but there were disputes about land and water rights, sometimes a bit of cattle rustling. (One fellow asked his neighbor, nice as pie, to borrow his truck one night, then used it to go steal cattle—that's the guts of a burglar: Sheriff Harry Morgenstern caught him at the auction house, with the check still in his pocket, and Bob sent him up the river.) There was always farm thievery and the usual run of drunk and disorderly. . . . In the beginning, Bob would generally go home for lunch, then be back for the afternoon, when he'd go home again, then he'd be back in the office at night. Evenings, he'd try to do his private work: wills and license applications that the farmers brought in. Bob never charged them much—maybe five or ten dollars. He needed friends more than money: there was always another election in two years. Springtime, they'd bring him their tax returns, and Bob would fill them out ("How many those steers d'you sell last fall? . . .") for two bucks, or even free. There was one CPA in Russell, but he had his hands full with the bankers and the oilmen. And Bob didn't mind. He had the time—or he made it. At Dawson Drug, when Chet and Bub would get the fountain clean, get the floor swept and the door locked, maybe eleven at night, they could always look down Main Street and see Bob's light in the courthouse.

Phyllis didn't mind, or said she didn't. She kept busy—in two or three bridge groups. She got Bob to go with her to a Sunday night game, and he was good, but after a while, he didn't have time. They rented a house on Sixth Street, and Phyllis had that to fix up: she did it early American, with stuff all stenciled and hand-painted like they did in New England. No one in Russell had ever seen its like. Phyllis taught some crafts to the local ladies—ceramics: no one in Russell had used that word before. Of course, there were friends, too, and family—Bob's family. Sometimes Phyllis would fill in alone, at Bina's house, for Sunday dinner, or potluck; Bob was working. Bina and Phyllis got along fine. Phyllis even learned, in time, how to make fried chicken. When all that wasn't quite enough, Phyllis took a job, part-time, at a florist's. Bob wasn't happy about that. In those days, if your wife went to work, it said something about you, as a man. But he didn't say anything. It'd be different . . . if they had kids.

It seemed like they never were going to have a child. Phyllis got herself tested, and the doctors didn't see anything they could do. Bob was always ready, in those days, to fear the worst about his own body, and one time, he went all the way to Chicago for tests. (Dr. Kelikian set that up.) But none of the doctors could say what the problem was—if there was a problem. After a while, they figured it just wasn't in the cards . . . maybe they'd adopt, but for that you had to do a home visit, it was part of the routine with the agency in Topeka—and that cost money, and . . . well, it dropped through the cracks, for a while.

Anyway, it wasn't like Bob had time to sit and worry. It seemed like he was always pushing harder, just to see how much he could do. Sometimes, he and Phyllis would go to someone's house for dinner, or bridge, and, come eleven, Bob would stand up and say he had to get back to the office. After midnight—till the bars on the highway closed—Sheriff Morgenstern would drive around, nab a drunk driver or two. And generally, when he got them back to the courthouse, he'd find Bob still at his desk. They'd book the drunks and arraign 'em, right there, 2:00 A.M. . . . Bob figured it was his job to get those cases out of the way. That's how he met Huck Boyd. Huck was a small-town newspaper editor and a Republican bigwig—National Committeeman for the state of Kansas. Anyway, one night Huck was driving through, on his way home to Phillipsburg, in northwest Kansas. Must have been midnight, and Huck looked up, saw a light in the courthouse. He thought there must be a break-in . . . got out of his car and went to investigate, and he found young Bob Dole, working at his desk. County Attorney . . . at midnight! Huck told the story to friends around the state. Meanwhile, he marked that boy Dole as a comer.

That he was. Summertime, when the farmers were lined up with the harvest on Main Street, Bob'd work his way down the row of trucks, just like he used to for Dawson Drug, except this time, he was only saying hello, shaking hands. Sometimes, he wouldn't even make it home for meals—he'd stay downtown for lunch with Harry, the Sheriff, then catch dinner at a Legion affair, or the Rotary. Sometimes, Phyllis used to say, it was like they didn't have time to talk . . .

"What do you wanna talk about?" Bob would say.

She didn't ask about his work. She got that piece of advice from another lawyer's wife. Doc Smith's wife: "Sometimes, it's better not to know." So Phyllis steered clear of his work life. It was just . . . that didn't seem to leave any life for her. When she did catch him, long enough to have a conversation, it was generally whether they were going this weekend to someone's house for dinner, or when Bob was going to get home that night. To which Bob would issue his standard reply, which was: "Depends."

Depends on what?

"On a lotta things."

Thing was, everyone talked about how well Bob was doing: Bina, the Dawsons, the old crowd in general. And Phyllis, for her part, certainly wasn't going to complain: she told her mother, who came to visit, that she loved Kansas—the people in Kansas. Her mother, Estelle, couldn't stand the place—it gave her the creeps, driving through the flat emptiness, past nothing but a thousand telephone poles, and then, on one pole, you'd see a sign: CITY LIMITS. How could you live like that? One time, Estelle and Phyllis's dad drove through Russell, all the way to Denver, and when Estelle came back she announced to the Doles: "Now I understand that cowboy music . . . it's nothing but a howl of human loneliness."

Phyllis was lonely sometimes, too, but she did what she had to—she found plenty to do. One springtime, she devoted weeks to learning how to make sugar Easter eggs. They were tiny, ornate, something she'd never seen before. Finally, one night, when Bob was home for dinner, she showed him: "Look, aren't these wonderful?"

"Yeah," he said, "was it worth walkin' on sugar for two weeks?"

It would be different, she thought, if they had a family. So they filed the papers to adopt in Topeka, but it took a long time, more than a year . . . and by that time, Phyllis found out she was pregnant. Bob and Phyllis had a little girl, whom they named Robin. And Bob was very pleased. He even came home in the evenings, for a while.

1 9 6 1

In the spring of '61, just after Bob got to D.C., JFK invited the freshmen in Congress to a dinner and reception. Phyllis was so excited—the White House! She set about making a new dress, in chintz with blooming roses, one of those wonderful sixties shapes with a high waist, straight skirt, a bow on the front. It was gorgeous! . . . But then Bob wouldn't say if they could go!

"Depends."

"Bob! on *what?*"

"Lotta things."

Bob had just been elected president of the House GOP freshmen. He didn't know if he was *supposed* to go to Democrat parties—even at the White House.

Phyllis didn't get an answer until that night: Bob showed up at their tiny house in Arlington, with a rented tux.

"Agh, we readyy?"

They drove to the White House in the Chrysler—then drove around trying to find the right gate. Marines in high-collar dress-blue tunics saluted them up the stairs, through the ceremonial entrance. In the Grand Foyer, the Marine Band, in white dinner jackets, serenaded the swirl of guests.

"I want to dance," Phyllis said. "I want to tell my grandchildren that I danced at the White House."

Bob and Phyllis stood with the other freshmen from Kansas—four of the six from their state were new. And when a sudden silence fell, and the Marine Band struck up "Hail to the Chief," the Doles and the others took one or two instinctive steps back, as the President and Mrs. Kennedy swept into the room.

There was no receiving line, no order, just everybody milling around in a sea of laughter, greeting, smiles. The Kennedys moved through the crowd with no apparent plan, yet they seemed to meet everybody. They were so gloriously at ease.

"Good evening, Mr. President," said one Kansas GOP freshman. "I'm Bob Ellsworth, from Kansas."

"Oh, yes," said Kennedy, like he'd been waiting all night to meet the Congressman from Lawrence. He turned to Jackie and said: "Dear, this is Vivian and Bob Ellsworth from Kansas." The Ellsworths were floored. The President knew Vivian's name! "Oh, yes!" said Jackie. "I'm so glad to meet you."

Then they were gone.

Bob's meeting was even briefer—a quick handshake in the hallway—the President had to leave early. (Turned out, that was a terrible night: the invasion of the Bay of Pigs.)

But Phyllis did have her dance in the White House. And Bob danced with his colleagues' wives, too. That night, the Marine Band played a song, "Mr. Wonderful," in honor of the new Commander in Chief. Rose Mary McVey, wife of Walter, the freshman Rep from Independence, said, "Oh, Bob, isn't it perfect?"

"Live it up while you can, Rose Mary," Dole advised. "We're parked in a ten-minute zone."

———————

Glorious ease was not Bob's style. Another man might have taken a deep breath and told himself he'd arrived—a member of Congress at thirty-seven, president of his class in the Capitol. Not Dole. What he remembered from that election among the freshmen was that he'd *fought* to beat Clark MacGregor, from Minnesota—by *one vote!* MacGregor'd prob'ly never forget! . . . It was too easy for Dole to see the matter through MacGregor's eyes (or as he imagined MacGregor must see it): Who is this rube from Dust-burg, Kansas?

It was a heady climb for anyone coming to Congress at that moment, when Washington seemed to hold not only power but promise of brilliance, glamor, and grace. There was money coursing through the government's pipes, and people who'd spend a private fortune on those with their hands on the spigot. There were lobbyists inviting them to parties, two or three *every night*—they really *ought* to go . . . and Washington hostesses— they loved these powerful young men. (Some ladies took liberties you'd seldom see in Kansas.) . . . All at once, there were reporters who wanted to know what these fellows thought—and cameras, TV cameras, and people holding doors for them, literally bowing them down the hallways of the Capitol.

Dole barely noticed this stuff.

Walter McVey, Rose Mary's husband, went off the deep end. He'd go to twenty parties in a week. He'd end up weary, pressed for time, not knowing where or who he was, yelling at some poor elevator operator, "Let's go! Don't you know who I am? I'm Congressman McVey!"

Walter was a smart man, a good lawyer, who served the southeast section of the state. Dole liked him; but he couldn't understand why Walter couldn't see himself. Dole was embarrassed when anyone held an elevator for him, or put him on a plane ahead of other folks. Bob was embarrassed for Walter McVey. . . . By the end of their first year, Walter had taken up with a secretary in his office. Rose Mary went home and filed for divorce. And that was the end of McVey. In another year, he lost his seat. People didn't like how he behaved. He forgot himself.

———————

Dole could not forget how he'd fought to get to Washington—*had* to fight! He had a primary against Keith Sebelius, a popular attorney from Norton, Kansas. Sebelius had run before, in '58, and come within an eyelash of knocking off the incumbent, a giant in that district, Wint Smith.

Dole stayed loyal to Wint in '58—Wint had done him some favors, sent him some law books (members of Congress got two copies of the Federal Statutes, each year) . . . and Bob Dole was a loyal young man. Anyway, Wint told him that '58 would be his last turn. Then, too, Bob figured if Sebelius got in, he'd be there for years. So Dole, the four-term County Attorney, was the man who delivered Russell County for Smith. . . . Wint held off Sebelius by a margin of fifty-one votes.

And that's when it started for Bob. Two years before his 1960 race, he was already meeting the powers in the big Sixth District, showing Wint's troops that Bob Dole could lead. That meant Bob had to show he was as tough as Wint ("the General" thought *Ike*, for Christ's sake, was namby-pamby on the commies). . . . Meanwhile, Dole started driving . . . twenty-six counties, from Salina west to the Colorado line, and all the way north to Nebraska—Dole hit every town, every country store, every café and filling station.

He ran the campaign from the basement of his home. Friends from Russell would crowd in, Friday nights, to drink Phyllis's coffee and get their assignments for the weekend. They weren't helping because they thought Bob was going to win—no one from Russell ever won anything—it was just that Bob was working so hard.

The problem wasn't only Sebelius (though Keith was problem enough—ex-commandant of the American Legion, which meant he had friends in every county post) . . . there was a third guy in the race, a State Senator named Phil *Doyle* . . . Doyle, Dole, Philip, Phyllis—it was murder!

That's how Bob started with the juice—Dole (not Doyle) Pineapple. The ladies from Russell would ride in the caravans, cutting up Dole-for-Congress labels and pasting Bob's name on paper cups. When they hit the next town, they'd set up a table on the courthouse square, or a Main Street sidewalk, and fill the cups with pineapple juice from blue-and-yellow Dole cans. After a while, they bought out the warehouse, they had to use Libby's juice. But that was their little secret—they washed out the Dole cans and refilled them with Libby's.

Then Phyllis made sixteen red felt skirts for the Dolls for Dole—each with a blue elephant (trimmed with sequins), and on the elephant's trunk, lettering that read, "Dole for Congress" . . . but not just that, there was a banner across each skirt: ROLL WITH DOLE. That *oh* was the crucial vowel!

That's why it was perfect when Leo Meyer and Fay built that Conestoga wagon, a scale model you could take apart and put in the trunk of a car (Kenny had to beg or borrow a big car because the wagon only fit in a Lincoln or Cadillac)—that was

the Roll-with-Dole wagon . . . and Fay's two girls each got skirts
from Phyllis that said I'M FOR ROBIN'S DADDY! so they could ride
the wagon, while the men, in red clip-on Roll-with-Dole ties,
pulled it up Main Street or rode it on the back of Harlan
Boxburger's flatbed, while Bob walked along, if it was a parade—Bob always walked in parades.

That's why he had his girl singers, whom Dole called the
Bob-o-Links—though sometimes they were introduced as the
Dolls for Dole Quartet—college girls who sang harmony (to the
accompaniment of a ukulele) on Bob's theme song:

> *Everyone here*
> *Kindly step to the rear . . .*

Which let people know that *Bob Dole was coming!* That was the
point: Bob was afraid that people wouldn't notice he was out
there!

And that was certainly the point of Bob's appearance at
Kansas Day, an annual GOP affair in the Jayhawk Hotel in
downtown Topeka, where the faithful stood around sipping
Cokes in the public rooms while the nabobs held court, with
stronger drink and cigars, upstairs. All in all, a staid affair, mid-
winter, gray, like the snow outside—until Bob Dole showed up,
with his wagon Roll-with-Doleing through the lobby, and the
Bob-o-Links in red Roll-with-Dole skirts hammering at their
ukulele, and twenty men and women all dressed up to Roll with
Dole, descending in ranks down the Jayhawk's grand staircase,
singing:

> *Everyone here*
> *Kindly step to the rear*
> *And let a winner lead the way! . . .*

And then, there was a young man riding a Dole unicycle through the crowd; and a Russell farmer dressed in an elephant's head; and eight pallbearers toting an open coffin, in which sat Frankenstein's Monster, bearing a sign: YOU HAVE NOTHING TO FEAR WITH DOLE.

People noticed.

In fact, they talked about nothing else that day, save the young fellow from Russell (There he is! . . . "Bob Dohhlll! Goodta meetcha!") who had such a tough primary, against Sebelius—but, well . . . looked like he might have a shot!

To the other candidates at the Jayhawk, here was something to fear: Dole was a palpable energy force in that hotel. He was throwing himself at that crowd with such abandon, it was almost frantic. Bob Ellsworth saw Dole for the first time that day, and thought no other politician would have done that—maybe they couldn't have. Dole was turning himself inside out.

Of course, Sebelius wasn't standing still. As commandant, he had a list of American Legion members, and he was using it for mailings . . . almost drove Dole crazy, the unfairness: *Bob* was a Legion man! And Doran before him! Why shouldn't *Bob Dole* have the list, too? He complained to the Legion. He argued that the bylaws prohibited help to any candidate. He threatened a legal challenge. He whined and wailed about this in the newspapers, in speeches. By the end of the campaign, the issue did Dole more good than any list.

By the end, there would be other mailings, too. Kansas was teetotal country—home of Carry Nation. (Bob used to joke, the Women's Christian Temperance Union was the only union that ever endorsed him.) . . . So imagine the impact, when all those letters arrived, revealing that *Sebelius was a lush!*

Keith's own mother was a life member of the WCTU. She

got a letter (with a Washington State postmark) that said her son was an alcoholic. She was in tears, and Keith was so enraged, he was close to crying, too. His mother had been a widow since Keith was six. He'd never do anything to disappoint her. Keith said to his wife, Bette: "If a guy wants an office this bad . . . well, it just isn't worth it." Of course, he assumed it was Dole's people doing the mailing.

Dole denied that.

Thing was, people knew Keith would take a drink—so it hurt him. No one could say how many votes it meant. All they could say was, in the end, some nine hundred votes separated Dole from Sebelius . . . and that sent Bob to Washington.

━━━━━

Anyway, Dole felt right away he had to make a splash! (Within two years his district would be combined with another—he'd have a Democrat incumbent as an opponent and *fifty-eight* counties to cover.) . . . So, before Bob and Phyllis settled into their rented house, off Lee Highway in suburban Virginia . . . before Phyllis had time to unpack all the linens and dishes she'd brought from Russell in the U-Haul (Bob flew ahead—didn't have time to drive) . . . and after Bob saw his first inauguration (it snowed the night before—Bob slept in the office and went in a shirt he bought at Drugfair) . . . after Bob set his office in the Cannon Building to cranking out mail, with the help of Wint Smith's old AA and a couple of gals from Russell . . . and as soon as he found his seat in the Ag Committee room and learned how to sprint from there to the floor . . . right away, he was on a plane again—back to Kansas.

In those days, the government paid for one or two trips home each year. Dole was back and forth every couple of weeks . . . and he sent out his newsletter every month (edited that himself), and handled his own press . . . and he was on the phone to Kansas every day, working his mail every night. He signed every letter himself. Most he dictated himself. And then, in careful lefty print, he'd write on the bottom—just a few words—or he'd send along a picture and he'd write on that. He sent Aunt Mildred a picture of himself, smiling on the Capitol steps, and wrote: "Finally made it. Lots of Democrats here."

Too many Democrats: they controlled the House, the Senate, and the White House.

There were a couple of ways a GOP freshman could handle this. Bob Ellsworth worked on flood-control projects. Those bills would sail through, with the backing of the aged Democrat lions—Jamie Whitten from Mississippi, George Mahon from Texas. Ellsworth could just hang on for the ride, make sure his district got its share. Dole's district didn't care about flood control; ag was all, and Bob was fixated on the farm bill. But even on the Ag Committee, Dole wasn't interested in playing ball. He was interested in showing that JFK, LBJ, and (the Ag Secretary) Orville Freeman—all those Democrats and their bureaucrats—were going to be the death of American farming, of American farmers, their families, and all that was good and holy wherever God caused wheat to sprout.

JFK was the President of eastern monied interests—which *always* put the shaft to the heartland farmer.

The liberals in Washington were going to run this country *commie.*

Orville Freeman, for pity's sake, wanted to send our wheat to the *Russians!* (What's the point of fighting them and feeding them at the same time?)

Dole never missed a vote. He had the highest ratings from

conservative "watchdog" groups—the antitax antidebt crusaders. He had one of the lowest ratios of support for the New Frontier. All this was in line with the views of Western Kansas. But Bob, being Bob, was sure it wasn't enough.

In the summer of '61, he and Phyllis went home to touch base . . . and Bob announced that Phyllis and Robin would stay, for a year and a half—keep the home fires burning while Bob took care of business in Washington.

That fall, Bob flew back and took care of JFK's Agriculture Department. There were stories in the paper from Pecos, Texas, about a wheeler-dealer good-ol'-boy (friend of LBJ's, matter of fact) who'd made a shady fortune storing grain for the government. This fellow's name was Billie Sol Estes.

Billie Sol was a man who knew a good deal—and what he had with the feds was a good deal. Say you had a grain elevator that was sitting empty . . . Estes would buy it—give you a good price—all in notes, understand, entirely on credit . . . after which, trains would start rumbling in with government surplus to fill the elevator. The government fees would pay off Billie Sol's notes, and everybody was happy—save for the fellows who used to store the grain, and a couple of spoilsport Ag Department guys who didn't think Estes should be storing every bushel the U.S. government bought. From '59 to '61, Estes stored 50 million bushels of grain and collected $8 million from the Ag Department . . . so taxpayers might have been unhappy, too—if they'd known.

They might never have known if Estes hadn't got himself in trouble with some bankers in Texas and Oklahoma who'd given him mortgages on 33,000 liquid-fertilizer tanks—when he owned, in total, only 1,800. (Billie Sol would just change the numbers on the tanks, depending on which bankers were coming that day.)

At the same time, Estes was buying cotton allotments from farmers in the Old Confederacy and transferring these allotments to his lands in West Texas . . . which wasn't much good, as cotton land went, but price supports were so inflated that an allotment (in effect, a license to grow cotton) was like a license to print money. Anyway, there was an Ag Department man in Texas named Marshall, and he refused to approve these cotton transfers. Marshall ended up dead on his ranch: he'd been poisoned with carbon monoxide, beat over the head, and gut-shot five times (with his own bolt-action .22 rifle). Still, taxpayers might never have known. Henry Marshall's death was ruled a suicide. After that, Estes's cotton assignments went through.

But after that, the case was in the papers, too, and the smell of ink reached Bob Dole in Washington.

Bob's fellow freshmen thought he must be crazy: What did Dole know about Billie Sol Estes? Bob was messing with the White House—with LBJ's friends! Dole was going to get clobbered!

But Dole called in the Attorney General of Texas—got him into the office and started finding out about the case. ("Duck soup!") . . . A friend at the RNC put Bob in touch with Ag Department sources—holdovers from Ike's regime who'd blow the whistle. . . . There was one Ag guy, M. Battle Hales, who'd accused Estes of buying off the department. Hales was reassigned—his office was locked and he was denied access to his own files. His secretary was shipped off to a mental institution. That's when Dole brought the matter to the floor—and to the papers. He wanted the Ag Committee to hold hearings. He wanted Hales to testify. He wanted to know where Orville Free-man had squirreled away Hales's secretary. These were the sorts of shenanigans by which the American farmer was bilked!

In the end, Bob Dole, freshman from Kansas, was the principal sponsor of the resolution that committed Congress to an investigation.

Bob Dole, freshman from Kansas, socked the Kennedy White House with its first taste of scandal.

Bob Dole, freshman from Kansas, made the case for the Republican Party, and the American farmer . . . in *The New York Times*.

"Agh, pretty *goood!* Front payyge!"

1968

The minute he got to Washington, Dole was a marked man. His district, which was already huge, was going to be combined with Floyd Breeding's—a Democrat! Dole had to fight to survive!

But he toughed it out, he *worked* his way back.

Two years later, his race was even harder. Had to fight his way through the Goldwater disaster. Pulled it out by his fingernails, and five thousand votes—five or ten votes in every town, he had hit them all . . . in a district as big as New York State . . . driving all night toward the next lights on the prairie, with one big fear:

Flat tire.

What the hell would he do?

Of course, no one knew that . . . Dole wouldn't talk about that.

No one knew either what it took to get dressed—those mornings on the road. Bob could use a buttonhook for the shirt now, but the top button might take a half-hour—and still might not work. He'd tie his tie himself now, even if Phyllis was around—but he might tie it five times. Had to be just so.

Nobody knew how he had to do his letters. Thousands of letters—he dictated every one, every word. Then Judy Harbaugh would bring them in and hold them on the desk while Dole signed with his left hand . . . until he told her, one day: "I'll do it."

He lifted his right fist onto a corner of a letter, and held the paper himself. It was awkward. But he wouldn't let her help anymore. "There's so many things I can't do," he told her. "I've got to try something every day, just to see if I can."

He didn't expect anything to come easy.

He sure wasn't going to sit still in the House. He had a chance now, and he took it: Kansas's senior Senator, Frank Carlson, announced that he'd retire in 1968 . . . same day, Dole announced he was running for Senate.

He'd have a primary against a man who'd already run statewide and won—the former Governor, Bill Avery, a friend of Dole's (they'd served together in Congress) and a big name.

It would be tough.

Well, you had to be tough!

Actually, it could have been tougher: Dole might have had to face Garner Shriver, another Congressman who'd run a dozen times—never lost—in Sedgwick County, Wichita. Garner owned that part of the state.

But Garner dithered, then backed away. Nobody could figure . . . what did Dole say to Shriver to push him out of the race?

"No, he never talked to me," Shriver recalled. "Uh . . . you see, he had this war record. Well, I did, too . . . but I didn't have this, uh . . ."

Shriver cocked his arm at his side: " . . . that was, uh, very visible."

In the end, it wasn't even Bob's arm. Had more to do with stomach. Garner had watched Dole in Congress.

"I don't think I had the desire he had. . . . I just didn't have all that push."

———————

People said Bob campaigned for that Senate seat like his life depended on it. Avery was well known (he'd won the governorship in '64 despite Goldwater's loss of Kansas by eighty thousand votes) . . . and Dole's name was new to most voters. Bob had to get around and make himself known—in a hurry!

He had a driver now, Bill Frazier, and they must have done a hundred thousand miles around Kansas. Frazier was a three-hundred-pounder, a trencherman, a smoker and drinker . . . but just the kind of guy Dole tended to rely on—big, ugly, and humble. He'd drop out of school every time Dole had a campaign. Probably never did finish school.

Anyway, it was always Dole and Frazier—they'd hit every wide place in the road. Dole only knew one way to campaign. He'd glad-hand his way up Main Street, on his way to a coffee-klatsch . . . if it was a big town, he'd start with coffee at some supporter's home, just to work up steam for the big event, at a rented hall. If it was a large hall, he might hook up with his quartet of girl singers, the Bob-o-Links . . . or his bevy of booster ladies, the Dolls for Dole—with their pineapple juice . . . or maybe he'd send brother Kenny ahead with the old "Roll with Dole" wagon. . . . Anyway, by the time Bob hit that hall, *he'd* be rolling—cracking jokes, telling stories, making up his speech on the spot . . . by the end, he'd be flying, barking out names, greetings, grabbing hands, chuckling for photos, moving through the crowd like a big steam engine. . . . Then he'd sink, in silence again, into the shotgun seat next to Frazier, and a hundred miles might go by before either one said a word.

Still, he talked to Frazier more than to anyone—who else did he have to talk to? . . . Phyllis would come along for the big events, but they weren't her happiest evenings. You'd see her near Bob (not too near), with an edgy smile . . . unless she saw someone she knew—then she'd light up. But there weren't many she knew. (It always made her feel inadequate: she couldn't remember all the names, and a *microphone*—oh, God!—*petrified* her.) She'd never tried to be Bob's partner in politics. How could she start now? . . . She told him she didn't like that "Dolls for Dole" routine anymore—made her think of *Valley of the Dolls*. . . . Of course, Bob kept the gals. He wasn't much for advice.

Dole knew the Senate was the big league, so he hired a *consultant*, a guy named Roy Pfautch. Dole listened to him for about two weeks, then tuned him out. Never fired him, of course. He'd just stop listening . . . joke about the guy, behind his back.

Dole still talked to Huck Boyd; Huck was always there for Bob. But despite his national connections, Huck was a man of western Kansas—northwest Kansas, to be precise—and never had as much drag with the eastern Kansas nabobs, the old guard: Alf Landon, Oscar Stauffer, or Harry Darby, the Kansas City boss. That was Dole's problem. His district covered half the state, but the wrong half, the empty west. Nobody knew Dole in the cities—Wichita, Topeka . . . Kansas City! What could he do in Kansas City?

He'd have to put it together by himself—go around the old guard. Outflank 'em, outwork 'em. He scheduled big events in all three cities—fund-raisers, hundred dollars a plate—and he went major-league. He hired a famous singer—well, pretty famous—Marilyn Maye, to sing Bob's theme song, "Step to the Rear (and Let a Winner Lead the Way)." She had it in her contract, she had to be introduced as "Marvelous Marilyn Maye." Bob did that . . . but after Topeka, she announced she couldn't be bothered to go on. Bob had to hire a big band—in a hurry. He *lost* money on Kansas City.

The problem wasn't really Kansas City. That was Wyandotte County—mostly black, not a factor in a GOP primary. The problem was in neighboring Johnson County, the most Republican county in eastern Kansas . . . a political jungle—twenty-five separate municipalities, each with its Mayor and City Council, and all well-to-do suburbs, foreign turf to Dole. Those people spent more time in Chicago, or New York, than they ever did in Russell, Kansas.

Dole found a way: he found a guy—Dave Owen. Owen was a comer, running for State Senator. He had that county wired. By the time he'd put together his organization and held a big party at a hotel to show it off, nobody would even file against him. So Owen turned his organization over to Dole—whole hog. . . . Why?

"I don't know, I met him . . . ," Owen said. "He had hero written all over him. He overcame his injuries. He never said a word about it. . . . I liked his style. There was something macho about him. He was kick-ass-and-take-names. Bob Dole stood for that."

So he did.

Dole's friend Bill Avery had lost the governorship, after one term, because he'd imposed a new income tax. The Democrats killed him, in '66, with that tax issue.

And so in the summer of 1968, when polls showed Dole flagging ("Gagh! What're we gonna *do*?") . . . he took a page from the Democrats' book:

Avery had the state studded with his trademark signs, verticals:

A

V

E

R

Y

. . . down the sides of a thousand telephone poles. So, every time Dole's workers found one of those poles, they tacked a horizontal sign on the bottom:

TAXES

By the day of the primary vote in August, it wasn't even close: Dole beat Avery two-to-one. Dole was going to the U.S. Senate.

1972

It was different for Dole in the Senate. Harder, in some ways. Not that he'd complain. He'd made it past . . . well, he never would have thought of himself in company with Calhoun, Clay . . . Daniel Webster! Dole felt he'd climbed higher than he ever had any right to dream.

No wonder he didn't have—couldn't have—the same ease that made him popular in the House . . . holding court at the snack bar in the House cloakroom (must have eaten five thousand of those Nutty Buddy ice-cream cones), wise-cracking with Helen behind the counter, making jokes about the members who were sprawled (some asnore) on the couches . . . you wouldn't see that in the Senate. It was so formal, the gentleman's club.

Dole didn't say a word on the floor for months. He didn't open his mouth . . . until April 14 of his first year: that was the anniversary of the day he was shot, a quarter-century past—on that day, Dole made his maiden speech, a plea for housing for the handicapped.

But once he started, he was hard to shut up.

The issue with Dole was the Vietnam War. That was an issue for everyone, of course, but Dole took it personally. Like the Democrats were trying to stick *him* with that failure, that suffering, those body bags. *His* Party hadn't started that war!

Dole had always backed the White House on Vietnam, but in a quiet way (House Republicans didn't have any choice— they were quiet). But this was different: a different forum for Dole—everything he said made news; a different climate on the war—moratorium marches filling the Mall, and the jails. Most of all, a different White House.

Dole had such respect for Richard Nixon, it was near reverence. Nixon had come to Kansas to campaign for Dole in '66. Dole would never forget their talk—how Nixon said the GOP would make stunning gains in the House that fall. The Party was flat on its back after Goldwater . . . but *Nixon called it*— within two or three seats! Dole had never seen anyone who knew politics like Nixon: he had the whole country at instant command in his head.

But it was more than that. In Nixon, Dole saw a man who'd been knocked down by life. But he was too tough to stay down. He started in a dusty California farm town . . . times were bad: story was, the family made it through the week eating ketchup. That meant something to Dole . . . and to Nixon, who never forgot where he'd come from . . . who *could not forget* that he never grew up with the world on his side—like, for instance, a *Kennedy.* . . . Dole understood, very well.

He saw strength in Nixon, and nobility: Dole mentioned once that Nixon was the only one in Washington who stuck out his left hand to shake with Dole. *The only one.*

So, in the Senate, Bob Dole was The One for Nixon. Dole let

nothing pass, no remark against the President, or his adminis-
tration. They weren't going to get away with *that* while Bob Dole
was on the Senate floor.

And he was on the floor, more and more. Dole thought he
saw the lay of the land: no first-termer could make hay in committee, not in the Ag Committee, not the most junior member of
the Senate's minority Party . . . but on the floor, it was wide
open! Hell, half the time you could shoot off a cannon and not
endanger one Republican life. . . . So Dole made the Senate
floor his preserve, his patrol.

Democrats were his targets. Dole never ceased to remind
them: it was *their* Party got us into Vietnam—another *Democrat
war!* . . . Richard Nixon (with his "Vietnamization") was only
trying to clean up *their mess!* . . . With his prairie voice rasping
resentment and scorn, Dole called the antiwar Senators "a
Who's Who of has-beens, would-bes, professional second-
guessers, and apologists for the policies which led us into this
tragic conflict in the first place."

Dole accused Ted Kennedy (his favorite target) of "the
meanest and most offensive sort of political distortion." . . .
Meanwhile, Dole accused Democrats of "parroting the propa-
ganda of a *communist enemy.*"

Well . . . the Kansas GOP hadn't sent him to compete for
Miss Congeniality.

In some ways, he was tougher on his GOP colleagues. He
wouldn't just answer them on the floor—he'd argue in the *cloakroom!* Demand to know what got into them. He couldn't understand why they wouldn't stand up for the President—the
Commander in Chief. Some of them were ducking and dodging
on the war . . . some who called themselves *leaders* were just as
bad as the Democrats!

Hugh Scott, who ran for Minority Leader (when Dirksen died, in '69)—there was a perfect example. Scott was an old windbag from Philadelphia (he came to Congress before Dole even got his first bus ride from the Army) . . . he was one of those eastern Rockefeller gents who never failed to get under Dole's skin. Scott was kissing up to the other side, spreading balm, playing the game.

This was no game, to Dole.

When a Young Turk named Howard Baker—a Tennessean, just two years Bob's senior in the Senate—challenged Scott for the Leader's job (Baker promised a more active, partisan attack), Dole backed him. Bob was out front for Baker!

That made an enemy of Scott, who won.

When Scott (and some other statesmen of the GOP—Dole could name them all) would not stand up for the President and his High Court nominee, Clement Haynesworth, Dole saw his duty: *he* took the floor. He accused Haynesworth's opponents of toadying to the liberal lobby. When they mentioned their duty to advise and consent, when they cited the Constitution, Dole stood up to retort: "It talks about *rights* in the Constitution—not about special-interest groups."

Well, he got noticed. . . . He was making hay, wasn't he? . . . First year in the Senate, he got ink by the barrel. ("Agh, pretty good! Front payyge!")

But in the Senate, there was a thin line between notice and notoriety. When someone asked Bill Saxbe, Republican of Ohio, to react to the latest broadside from Dole, Saxbe shrugged it off:

"Aw, Dole's just a hatchet man. . . . He's so unpopular, he couldn't peddle beer on a troopship."

Dole was stung—stunned, more like it. Of course, he knew it all came from Scott. When Scott farted, Saxbe stunk, but . . . *hatchet man?* Is that what they thought?

He said to his old House colleague, Bob Ellsworth, "And these are my friends?"

Ellsworth had Dole's thorough respect. They'd come to Congress together. After '66, when Ellsworth lost his bid for the Senate, he ended up working for Nixon as National Political Director—to Dole, an awesome credential. He used to say: "Ellsworth's smarter than the rest of us put together."

Now Ellsworth said to Dole: "Don't worry about them, Bob . . ."

Ellsworth thought Dole's problems came from being too hard-edged, too frantic. He only had to calm down.

"The shrubs are always attacking the roots of the oak," Ellsworth said. "They can't stand its being so tall and strong."

Well, Dole would stand his ground—tall and strong. He wasn't going to slink away to some corner, his tail between his legs, no. Sometimes you had to be tough!

The President understood! From time to time, in his second year, Dole would arrive at his office to find an envelope—from the White House! With a red tag—"Urgent!" Inside, there'd be a statement for Dole to read on the floor, a speech *for the President*. Dole would head for the chamber.

Then, too—more rarely—he was summoned to The Presence. The staff would buzz with the news all day. "Senator's going to the White House! . . . Dole's been invited by the President! . . ." This was heady business—though Dole tried not to show that.

One day, he did announce to his staff that next time, *he* would challenge Hugh Scott for the Leader's job.

"Senator, you can't do that."

"Why not? Jerry Ford did it in the House."

"But Senate's different—you gotta take some time, earn your way in."

"How do you do that?"

"Well, you know, Scott was already Party Chairman."

"Yeah . . . how do you go for Party Chairman?"

Turned out, you went by way of the White House—just the route Dole's duty had paved. There was talk that Rogers Morton would soon step out of the top Party job. Nixon's men wanted a kick-ass team for '72 . . . they needed someone who would *stand up for the President.*

John Mitchell told Dole in the first days of 1971: the job would be his—Chairman of the Republican National Committee.

Dole was moving fast, going national! (Who could tell what might happen now? Nixon might even get tired of dragging Agnew behind him!) . . . Dole told the good news to friends in Kansas, in Congress. . . . That's when Hugh Scott found out.

Scott protested to the White House, and within hours, other Senators weighed in, talking Dole down. (Publicly, Scott contended the job was too big for a sitting Senator—in private, he called Dole's selection a personal affront.)

H. R. Haldeman, the Chief of Staff, called Dole the next day, from San Clemente:

So sorry, Haldeman said. The President had changed his mind.

Dole was ashamed, enraged. How could they treat him like that? After his loyalty! . . . Did they expect him to go down without a fight? He found out that Nixon's palace guard was planning to install Tom Evans, from Delaware—an eastern money man! That night, Dole told his friend Bryce Harlow: if that's how Nixon's men meant to treat him . . . well, he didn't think he'd even stay in the Senate. Harlow told him to forget that whine . . . then he brokered a deal: Dole would get the chairman's job, but the White House would name Evans cochairman at the same time.

Dole refused.

If they had to have Evans, *Dole* would make the appointment. . . . There could be only one chairman!

Till 3:00 A.M., Dole hung tough. ("They're not gonna do this to me!") . . . In the end, he had to appoint two cochairs—Evans and Anne Armstrong, from Texas . . . but he won! Well—didn't he?

Bob Dole got the chairman's job.

He'd have a big press conference (biggest of his life!) to announce the glad news. . . . He was on the move!

What a shame, it left such a sour taste.

"I want out."

Dole got the big office on the top floor on First Street—the one with the grand desk, that huge map behind . . . ("Heyy! Nice digs!"), but his job was not to sit in the office.

He started crisscrossing the country, rallying for '72, raising money, trying to broaden the Party at its base. From the chairman's pulpit, Dole meant to open the Party to groups long-ignored: farmers, blue-collar ethnics . . . blacks, Mexicans, Asians . . . he never lost a chance to remind a crowd that his, *theirs,* was the Party of Lincoln, liberty, emancipation.

He never lost a chance at a crowd. Dole was determined to show his critics—show everyone—that he could carry his Senate load (he still never missed a roll call) and show up in every corner of the country to build the Party and its hopes for '72. Now, for the first time, a car came to fetch him, idling at the base of the Capitol steps as the Senate finished business for the afternoon . . . a jet was waiting at the airport . . . advance men were waiting at another airport one or two thousand miles to the west. If Dole could pick up a time zone or two on his way to the dinner, the funder, the rally . . . he might have time for a press conference, too—or a stop, somewhere, refueling. . . . "Agh, better make it Kansas."

Kansans are always schizoid when one of their own grabs a glimmer of limelight: they're *so* pleased (can't believe, you know, a guy from *Kansas*) . . . that they're instantly on guard for some *slight* (that guy doesn't care about *Kansas* anymore!). . . . There's a window of about ten days before they decide: *That fellow's got too big for his britches!* . . . So Dole would stop in Kansas, two or three times a week—every time his plane poked west of Ohio, he'd order his pilot to gas up in K.C. or Wichita, Salina or Great Bend . . . while he scooted for a half-hour, hit a Kiwanis, or cut a ribbon for a new mall.

Of course, it was midnight, or after, when he'd land again in D.C. (that's the bad news with time zones—you end up paying them back). Dole would have the car drop him at his big house on Beechway, in Virginia—tell the driver what time to come back. Bob would head for the basement. If Phyllis was still up, she might bring him dinner on a tray. That's when she'd say anything she had to tell him. Then she'd go upstairs. . . . Bob would sleep on his bed, in his cellar.

Chet Dawson made a visit to Washington that year, and he came back to Russell shaking his head: "Bob came home at 2:00 A.M.," Chet told the boys in the drugstore. "I guess he didn't want to disturb Phyllis, so he just curled up downstairs. Four hours later, the limo showed up to take him away again. . . . What kind of life is that?"

That's what Phyllis wanted to know. Sometimes, she'd bring Bob's tray, with his food—all cut up, as he liked it—and she'd muster courage to announce: "We have to talk."

Bob would snap: "Whaddya want to talk about?"

She never had a good answer. There was no answer short or neat enough. It was just . . . they had to talk—didn't they? . . . What happened to their life? If they couldn't talk, well . . .

It wasn't that they fought. (Bob didn't have time.) Sometimes, she would have liked a fight . . . then she could *scream* . . . maybe he'd see how she felt—see her. But when? . . . She tried to think of ways she could be different, to fit in with his life. Maybe she should stay up, eat supper with him. But Robin had to eat. And had to get to bed—Robin had school. Phyllis could count—she went back and *figured out*—how many times they'd had dinner together, the three of them, that year, when Bob made chairman. Two times.

One day Robin told her: "Mom, all my friends' parents sleep together."

Phyllis put on a brave face: "Well . . . you don't know what happens when you're asleep—do you?"

She would ever remember the day she knew that life with Bob was never going to "straighten out"—was never going to be the life she'd thought of as a girl in New Hampshire, nor even the life she'd had in Russell, Kansas.

It was the mid-sixties, Robin was in grade school, maybe eleven years old, and she had a doctor's appointment. The doctor was a wise old head who'd dealt with hundreds of young girls. . . . So, just to keep Robin from worrying while he made his examination, the doctor asked—would she like to have her ears pierced? He offered to do the job, thirty-five dollars, including gold posts . . . of course, he'd take care of any complications, infections, whatever . . . Robin should ask her folks.

Well, Robin came out of that office high as a kite—so excited! Could she get her ears pierced? . . . Mom? . . . Mom! Could she?

Phyllis didn't know what to say. (Where she grew up, the only young girls with pierced ears were gypsies . . . or, uh, worse!) "Well . . . ," she said, "you'll have to ask your father."

That night, Robin left a note in the basement.

"Dear Dad: Can I please, please, please, *please* have my ears pierced? I talked to the doctor and he said it would cost $35 and that would cover any complications. Please, *please* . . . Love, Robin."

And she drew, at the bottom, two boxes: One marked YES, and the other NO. At age eleven, she'd left her father a speed-memo.

(His response was also characteristic. He drew a third box, checked it, and marked it MAYBE. He scrawled underneath: "I'll talk to you Tuesday." That was three or four days away—for a girl that age, an eternity. Of course, when they did talk, he was a pushover. Phyllis had to take Robin to the doctor, get it done.)

Anyway, Phyllis knew then. When she saw how surely Robin knew her dad, when she saw how her daughter accepted the facts—the way Bob was . . . then Phyllis had to accept, too: it would never be as she had dreamed it would be.

She rolled with it. Or she thought she did. She tried. She'd say what she had to, in the basement . . . then she'd leave him alone. If they got a social invitation, she'd tell him, but she wouldn't push. Sometimes, she'd go to the parties alone. When she got to feeling guilty about always being the guest, she'd invite everybody for dinner, then tell Bob: he was having a party . . . did he want to come?

They did get along—they *never fought.* That's why she felt like she'd been kicked . . . when Bob said, one night, in the basement:

"I want out."

He wasn't happy. They could see that—the ones who knew him, staff who'd been with Dole since Kansas: they always knew—from the comments that leaked as he worked through the day, jokes he muttered after calls from the CREEPs. (It was Dole who gave Washington that nickname for the CRP, Nixon's Committee to Reelect the President.)

The problem was, the CREEPs held all the cards (and the money—Nixon's reelection budget was ten times bigger than the RNC's) . . . they treated the Republican Committee like a poor cousin . . . or worse: like a trained dog they had leashed in the backyard, to be loosed whenever Mitchell, Haldeman, or Colson yelled, *"Sic 'em!"*

That wasn't how Dole saw the job. He'd learned a few things after three years in the Senate—he had more respect for his colleagues, and himself.

Sure, he'd attack George McGovern in speeches—try to paint him onto the left-wing fringe . . . or off the edge of the canvas! But Dole wouldn't let the Party newsletter use the cartoon (Chuck Colson sent it over) showing McGovern in the black pj's of the Viet Cong. He wouldn't send out the letter hinting that Hubert Humphrey had a problem with booze. He wouldn't use the collection of new, kindly comments from Ted Kennedy about George Wallace (Colson's headline: WHAT A DIFFERENCE A BULLET MAKES!).

Most of the envelopes with the red tags ("Urgent!") ended up in Dole's wastebasket now. Dole knew they didn't come from Nixon.

Problem was, he didn't know what Nixon wanted. The minute Dole demonstrated his independence, he was adjudged "unreliable" by the CREEPs and the White House crowd. By '72, Dole couldn't get in to see the President . . . couldn't ask what Nixon wanted . . . couldn't ask for Nixon's help. That frustration leaked from Dole, too—in the usual way:

"Agh, I called Haldeman, I said, 'Bob, I'm the National Chairman! I want to see the President!'

"He said, 'Fine. Tune in Channel Nine at ten o'clock. You can see him then.'"

In fact, so painful and public was Dole's estrangement from the power crowd . . . it probably saved his career. When burglars broke into the Watergate office of the Democratic National Committee, Dole couldn't even take the story seriously. He'd never believe those Big Guys in the White House were involved.

He did ask his Big Guy friend Bryce Harlow . . . who couldn't make much of the story, either. "It's got no legs," Harlow said. "It'll blow over . . ." Dole thought he might make a formal statement—say the Party had nothing to do with this fiasco.

But that might look like he was backing away . . .

"It'll fade in two or three days," Harlow said.

Dole raised the subject, once, at the White House. "I'm getting questions on the, uh, Watergate," he said. "Maybe we oughta make a statement, just to clear the air." But that suggestion lay on the table like a dead fish. Nixon didn't say a word.

So, Dole saw his duty: he hit the road, tucked his head . . . handled the questions in his own way:

"Agh, well, we got the burglar vote . . . "

Dutifully, Dole swiped at *The Washington Post*: *The Post* was in bed with McGovern! Doing the Democrats' dirty work! . . . More than dutifully, Dole flew around the nation, trumpeting Nixon's achievements: revenue-sharing for the states; draft reform, a volunteer Army; the diplomatic opening of China; the hundreds of thousands of boys he'd brought home—with honor—from Vietnam. Dole did believe that Nixon was solving the problems that mattered to Americans, that McGovern was out of step . . . that Nixon would win by a landslide . . . that Nixon could *reorder* the nation's politics—not just in the White House, but in Congress, in the states.

But the CREEPs only cared about the reelection—a landslide for the President. They didn't want to hear about downballot races. Dole couldn't even get a call through to Nixon's *staff* anymore. They treated the Party like an *enemy.* What could Dole do?

He kept flying. When the Senate went into recess, he stayed on the road for weeks. If they scheduled him a day to rest, an evening home, he'd remind them of some commitment he'd made, some emergency in a distant state. He didn't want to go home.

One night in D.C., he sat up late, in half-darkness, in his Senate office. Staff was gone—except for Judy Harbaugh and his RNC driver, waiting for Dole to call it quits. "I want to talk to you," Dole told Judy. "I'm going to need your help."

Judy tried not to gawk. Bob Dole never asked for help.

"Looks like I'm going to get a divorce."

She didn't know what to say. She knew—they all knew in that office—Dole didn't have much family life. They always figured that was the way he was cut out. The shock was that he meant to do anything about it.

———————

It wasn't really what he meant to do. . . . After he said he wanted out, he didn't bring it up with Phyllis for weeks: they stuck to their routines. When Bob did try to talk to her again ("Well, we don't want lawyers gettin' their hands on everything—we prob'ly ought to talk") . . . it was too late.

"Here's the name of *my* lawyer," Phyllis said. "Talk to him."

Still, Bob didn't leave . . . he wouldn't go. He stayed at the house (as much as he stayed anywhere) all through the divorce. He didn't know where to go. It was Phyllis who finally called his RNC driver to come over and put Bob's belongings in the garage.

Bob told Judy Harbaugh: "I need you to find me a place to live."

She rented him a tiny place in the Sheraton Park hotel. She got him some linens, and kitchen stuff—plates, a couple of pans—so he could cook . . . if he could cook . . . what was he going to cook? For the first time in his life, Bob Dole was alone.

He hadn't felt like that since the Army, the hospitals. How could he end up like that again? . . . How could he not? He had no friends to call, no family in town. He couldn't even call his mother—Bina took that divorce hard. She took to the couch in the front room, in Russell. She blamed Bob . . . and herself. If she'd paid more attention to Phyllis—just a little more!—this wouldn't have happened. Never! She was so miserable. Doran couldn't even get her up for Christmas. Bina said: "There'll be no Christmas for me."

Phyllis's mom, Estelle, blamed her daughter. She thought Bob didn't really want to leave. She told Bob it would break her own heart if he went through with this, if he let Phyllis go. "Well," Bob replied softly, "if that's what she wants . . ."

The fact was, he had no idea how to work his will in a personal affair. Politics, sure—but not this . . . and not now. He was tired, stretched thin. He could not find the will.

He took sick, with a vicious infection that laid him out for days, while he thought what he might have said, or done— thought back through *years,* how it might have been different . . . but he could not make it different. He couldn't do any more now. He was in his bed . . . well, not his bed. It was that hotel, four walls . . . not much else.

———————

He had his job, thank God, and he did it. As soon as he was out of bed, he was in the air again—another coast-to-coast swing. Bob Dole wasn't the kind to quit. Sometimes, you had to be tough! He flew a quarter-million miles in that election, for the Party, for the President.

That year, '72, Nixon piled up the biggest margin of any Republican in history. Of course, the President and his men were exultant . . . though Nixon did, sure enough, fail to mention any Party institutions in his victory speech.

Only Dole seemed to notice that.

Sure enough, Nixon's landslide did not raise the GOP to power in either house of Congress. In fact, liberal Democrats unseated Republican Senators from Maine, Colorado, Delaware, and Iowa.

Only Dole seemed to harp on that.

That was his reputation, by that time, in the White House: sour all the way—Bob Dole, crying wolf for the Party. One week after election, the capital's smart-guy community knew: Dole was on his way out—just a question of when.

Dole didn't need the tom-toms to tell him . . . it was almost

time, anyway. He'd have his own reelection campaign in 1974.
If he could bow out of the chairman's job with grace—say, mid-
'73 . . . well, that would give everybody time.

Only Dole had grace in mind.

Two weeks after the election, Dole was summoned. It was
his first visit to Camp David—his last for many years. Nixon
had him flown up by chopper, with Attorney General Dick
Kleindienst—who looked like a man on the way to his hanging.
That's when Dole figured: maybe there was a noose for him, too.

Dole said, by way of small talk, "Agh, d'ya bring your
rope?"

But no . . . Nixon was awfully kind—talked about all the
work Bob had done—helluva job! . . . The President had that
big map from the office, all striped now with flight paths—that
was a gift for Dole. And a jacket, emblazoned: "Camp David."
Nixon couldn't have been friendlier—wanted to talk about
Bob's future.

"Well, I have been working hard," Dole allowed. "I thought
maybe I could stick around, have a little fun with the job, a few
months . . ."

Nixon was nodding: yes, he'd figured Bob was ready to
move on.

"No, well, I mean . . ."

No need to explain: Nixon understood! Well, who did Bob
think should be his successor? . . . Of course, Dole caught the
drift. He mentioned some Big Guys—Mel Laird might be
good. . . .

That's when Nixon brought up the name George Bush.
Nixon wanted to place Bush . . . but Bush didn't want to be
number two anywhere. Maybe he could be number one at the
RNC. Did Dole think Bush might take the job? . . . It was John

Mitchell who suggested that Dole go to New York, sound out Bush—see if he'd be willing.

So, dutifully, Dole flew to New York, had his meeting with Bush, took his sounding, in the Waldorf. . . . Bush was cordial—nice guy, you know—he listened, smiled, didn't say yes, didn't rule it out.

Dutifully, Dole reported back to the White House.

It was only later, after Dole found himself and his daughter in the *last car* of Nixon's inaugural parade (well, just about the last car—maybe some cops behind them, or a sanitation crew) . . . after Dole learned from the papers that he'd been dumped as chairman (his demise unceremoniously leaked) . . . along with the news that he'd been dumped for George Bush . . . did Dole learn that Bush had talked to Nixon.

Bush had talked to Nixon before Dole ever flew to New York!

You'd think Bush might have said—somehow, let Dole know—it was all just a dog and pony show . . . he'd already taken Dole's job!

"Gaghhd! Guy just sat there! . . ."

Nice guy!

Well, didn't matter anymore—did it? Dole's job was gone. He was back in that hotel, alone, with those walls . . . his map, a Camp David jacket in the closet . . . and in his head, an unfading memory of Bush's blank, friendly smile.

No Future at All

It dawned on Dole only slowly that he'd have to fight for his life—when Watergate burst open like a bad cantaloupe, when everything around him turned foul, all at once.

It wasn't that Watergate snuck up on him. He didn't try to wish it away, or deny its import . . . not anymore. Once he'd left the Party chair, there was no Republican more vocal, more candid about the scandal. Dole saw the cover-up killing Nixon's Presidency, and he knew Republicans would suffer, at the polls. Still, it was a stomach-turning shock to him—an affront—when they came at *him,* in Kansas!

It started with Norbert Dreiling, "Mr. Democrat," from Hays. Dole showed up in Kansas, around the turn of the year, 1974, for the first quiet *ta-rappa-tap-tap* of his reelection soft-shoe . . . and Norb was already slamming him with the portentous question:

What did Dole know, and when did he know it?

Either Dole was *culpable of knowing* (and was, therefore, like his President, an unindicted coconspirator) . . . or Dole (the National Chairman!) was *unaware, out of the loop* (therefore, impotent, imbecilic) . . . which would Bob have us believe?

Dole was so enraged by this line of inquiry that he threatened to *sue* . . . at which point Norb, a lawyer by trade and a brawler by temperament, replied in every Kansas paper: "Let him file his damn suit! Then he can answer the question under oath!"

Only the mildest stuff made it into the papers. As usual, in Kansas, the real poison was spread by word of mouth. People would take Dole aside, after events—these were supporters!—and quietly, half-ashamed, ask if it was true, what they heard:

"Bob, they say the burglars kept their tools at your apartment!"

Sure, that one was easy to knock down—Dole wasn't renting at the Watergate until the year after the burglary. But how could he tell that to the thousands who *didn't* ask? . . . As usual, Dole feared the things people would not say.

For instance, the divorce: no one brought it up with Dole. But *everybody knew,* of course, how Bob dumped that gal, Phyllis—you know, when he went fancy-pants, with Nixon . . . just as they knew that Phyllis was *his nurse* . . . nursed him back *from the dead* . . . now he didn't need her anymore, he . . . well, people knew how *that* went, with men. (Prob'ly got some chippy in that *Watergate—everybody* knew about *that* place!)

There was no way Dole could silence the whispers.

No more than he could shut down the standard Kansas whine: Bob Dole had been National Chairman—must not *care about Kansas* anymore. (Maybe that Dole's gettin' too big for his britches!)

He couldn't stop the cover-up from ruining his patron-

President . . . any more than he could stop Jerry Ford from issuing his pardon. (Someone asked Dole, after the pardon, whether he'd get campaign help from Ford. "I think Ford's given me 'bout all the help I can stand," Dole said.)

There was no way he could stop the Democratic Senatorial Campaign Committee from naming Kansas—him!—as a "vulnerable target" . . . sending money to fuel his opponent—his *respected* opponent, the Topeka physician and two-term Congressman, Bill Roy . . . any more than Dole could forestall Dr. Roy from stumping the state (to increasing approbation) for "integrity in government" and an "independent Senator for Kansas."

What could Dole do?

Well, he could use his new national connections to raise hundreds of thousands of dollars . . . which he could spend for *professional help*—high-tech consultants! He hired a Campaign-Manager-guru named Herb Williams ("Agh! Pretty *good*—guy worked for *Dann*-forth!") . . . Dole got a fast-talking pollster, Tully Plesser; a top-notch adman, Jack Connors, from Boston. . . . Dole had airplanes to fly him around the state—or *choppers!* . . . He would spare no effort, or expense.

Which made it all the more depressing, through that long summer of '74, as Dole's high-tech campaign ground to a bitter standstill in Kansas. The consultants couldn't get along with Kansans. Herb Williams proved he could handle a flowchart, rent offices, hire staff; he could denounce everyone else's ideas as bullshit, rend the air with a blue streak of oaths, work everyone around him to a frazzle, and spend a fortune—for nothing—or at least without benefit to Dole. (And Dole, of course, couldn't fire him—never fired anybody!) The highly creative admen in Boston had yet to produce a single ad. (They did design a handsome tabloid—printed tens of thousands—but they spelled Wichita *Witchita,* so those landed in the trash.) And Dr. Bill Roy (who began as an unknown in four-fifths of the state) drew even in the polls, and then pulled ahead, by five points, ten . . . by *thirteen points* (in Dole's own pricey polls!).

Dole knew, by that time, he was in a fight for his life. But he seemed like a boxer who'd been punched woozy in the ring. He wasn't quite sure how he'd got there . . . or what the hell to do to get out . . . he didn't seem to have any plan, any will, to pull out of his swoon tomorrow, next week . . . at any point in the future!

Dole couldn't convince himself that he had any future at all.

Elizabeth

Politics was the only part of his life that meant anything, that was left to him. But everything ended up looking wrong—he couldn't make people *see* . . .

The buzz in Congress that year, '74, was inflation: Whip Inflation Now! . . . That was the first time Dole put forth his instinctive notion that Congress (that he) could cut the budget fairly. But every finger of government, every program, would pay the price—say, five percent . . . just tighten up the belt! On the floor of the Senate, Dole proved his *bona fides* when he offered an amendment to cut five percent from the agriculture appropriation. "I offer this amendment," he said, "because every Senator's got to take the hit."

By the time Dole got back to Kansas, Bill Roy had the state half-convinced that Dole was *taking money from the farmers*— stealing the sneakers off their children's feet! Why would Bob Dole vote against his farmers?

Well, to serve his President, and Party . . . just as he opted for President and Party when he took the RNC chair . . . and forgot about Kansas, spent his time all over the country, making "hatchet-man speeches for Nixon." . . . Bob was a caustic fellow, anyway, and partisan, with those nasty jokes—not a caring man, like Bill Roy, who was a *doctor*, a healer (delivered five thousand babies!) bringing *life* . . . and then, in concern for the public weal, decided that he must study law, as well . . . which he did, at night, *with his wife* (who also became a lawyer) . . . Dr. Bill Roy was a man of concern, credentials, family, faith . . .

Bill Roy was about to bury Bob Dole.

At the start of September, Lieutenant Governor Dave Owen (he'd decided not to run for another term) became the working chairman of the Dole reelection campaign. In D.C., Dole's top Senate staffers quit the federal payroll to volunteer in Kansas. They found a campaign in ruins:

There were no ads, no money to run ads. (Dole had raised half a million dollars, but Herb Williams spent it. Dave Owen would find eighty thousand dollars in unpaid bills in Williams's credenza.) There were true Dole-folk all over the state, but they'd almost given up. The campaign was flirting with the fatal affliction: it was ridiculous. Williams and his high-tech campaigners had managed to contract for billboards . . . but no one had come up with art or copy—Dole was renting empty billboards.

Somehow, they had to get rid of Williams . . . but the campaign could not take another bad-news story. Somehow, they had to make some good news—some ads! . . . but where was the money?

Owen and friends called some guys together at the Petroleum Club—twenty or thirty good fellows—and walked out that same day with $130,000.

Then Owen called the ad agency in Boston and threatened

to start making ads himself. He did, in fact, hire a local announcer to sit on a stool, with a smoke in his hand, and stare straight into the camera while he took the hide off Bill Roy. (That was an old format used by Governor Bob Docking—it was ugly, but it'd worked before.) Jack Connors called from Boston, to protest: just hold on forty-eight hours! . . . Sure enough, on day two, Owen got tapes, air express.

The ads showed a standard campaign poster of Bob Dole, and off-camera, a narrator said:

"Bill Roy says Bob Dole is against the Kansas farmer." (FWAP . . . a big glob of slimy mud hit the poster, and slid down Dole's face.)

"Roy says Bob Dole voted to cut school lunches." (FWAP . . . another glob of mud.)

"Roy says Bob Dole voted against cuts in the federal budget." (FWAP . . .)

Then the announcer rebutted all the charges, and said Dole was *for* budget-cutting, school lunches, and the Kansas farmer. . . . Meanwhile, the film was reversed, the mud started flying off the poster, leaving a handsome and smiling Bob Dole.

"All of which makes Bob Dole look pretty good," the narrator said. *". . . and makes Bill Roy look like just another mudslinger."*

The ads caused an uproar. Kansans had never seen their politics played out so graphically. Half the voters thought these were Bill Roy's ads—they were furious: How could he fling that slime at Dole? The other half understood they were Dole ads—and they were mad at *Dole* for throwing mud at his own face! . . . Voters called the TV stations, wrote letters to the papers, they denounced dirty campaigning and candidates who sullied the airwaves—and Kansas!

Dole thought he had to pull the ads. (Of course, he wouldn't say that. He had Huck Boyd call Dave Owen to suggest that *Owen* ought to pull the ads.) But how could anyone pull the ads? Dole would look like a waffler! He'd look ridiculous!

Owen and the boys thought up the play:

First, Dole quietly reserved for Herb Williams a soft landing pad with the RNC in Washington. Next, Williams held a press conference—in Kansas—and quit Dole's campaign . . . because *Dole would not permit him* to run any more mudslinger ads.

Eureka! The ads came off the air, and Dole got rid of his Campaign Manager, six weeks before the vote. . . . But instead of two killer stories—DOLE CAMPAIGN IN DISARRAY—Dole got one plump creampuff: Bob was too nice, too honorable, for dirty politics.

In the end, it was Bill Roy who couldn't pull the trigger. The Democrats had prepared ads on Watergate—Dole as Dick Nixon's political twin and alter ego . . . but the state chairman didn't want to take the low road. So Roy held back the ads—despite warnings from Norb Dreiling, who knew Dole well. "You let Bob Dole get his head off the mat," Norb said, "and you'll never hold him down."

Then, too, the Roy campaign decided not to answer the antiabortion nuts. They were after Roy as an obstetrician who had performed abortions when the health of his patients required them. In fact, Roy had hated abortion since his residency in Detroit, when he watched a teenage girl die in his emergency room because a back-alley abortionist had perforated her uterus. But the Roy campaign decided not to "dignify" the issue. Abortion was a matter of medical ethics—and Roy was, first and foremost, a doctor. He'd jumped from medicine to Congress, in 1970, in a three-month campaign—politics was not his life.

He would find out, it was Bob Dole's life.

The great confrontation was the half-hour Agriculture Debate at the Kansas State Fair, in Hutchinson. Dole insisted on the Lincoln-Douglas format—no moderator, no panel, just the two candidates, toe-to-toe, in a tent, and on statewide TV. Both candidates tried to pack the arena. The Dole crowd, Russell folks, were *convinced* that Roy's people were nothing but thugs (who'd been *paid* ten dollars apiece to show up!). Those Roy people were cheering when their man asked Dole:

"Why did you support legislation to do away with the Department of Agriculture, when it's so important to the farmers of Kansas? . . ."

Dole didn't know what legislation Roy was talking about. (His staff had put together a fat briefing book—last minute, of course, dictated from phone booths—Bob never looked at it.) Dole hemmed and hawed: he couldn't answer, and that threw him off track.

Near the front of the crowd, Bina Dole kept her eyes on her son, and as he began to press, she saw his brow grow dark. She knew that look—he was enraged. Bina stopped whispering with the other Russell ladies, her own mouth drew into a tight line— she was rigid with worry, her hands worked in her lap. Bill Roy was pressing his advantage, painting Dole as a thoughtless political slasher . . . *Look who you are . . . compared to me—a doctor!*

How could Bill Roy know . . . that was what Bob Dole always wanted to be? How could Roy understand what had been stolen from Dole . . . as Roy seemed now to be stealing the rest of Bob's life?

With one minute left, Dole strode to the podium. "Why do you do abortions?" Dole said. "And why do you favor abortion on demand?"

There was an instant's hush in the tent . . . the crowd began to boo. This was so ugly . . . hundreds of people—not just Roy's crowd—were hooting Dole back to his chair.

Roy stammered out words, but nothing like an answer. He knew he had less than thirty seconds. The statewide broadcast ended with his senseless mumble into the microphone, the angry hoots of the crowd, and Bob Dole stalking off stage.

The folks from Russell planned to stay for dinner, but Bob didn't come. He had a plane waiting to take him to Parsons—just a three-seater. Dole asked Bill Wohlford: "Whyn'cha come on to Parsons?"

Wohlford was one of Dole's Washington staffers who'd quit his job to help in Kansas—one of those big, humble Dole loyalists who didn't expect much talk from the Senator. Wohlford hardly knew what to say in the plane—though he saw: Dole was down. For the first time that Wohlford knew, Dole seemed to want reassurance. It was dark in the plane—just dim nightlights, the glow from gauges . . . Dole was slumped in a slingseat.

"We can do it," Wohlford said, heartily. "We just got a lot of work, but we got a lot of people now . . . we just have to turn it loose!"

He meant, to win.

"Yeah," Dole said. " . . . I'm just not sure it's worth it."

In the end, there was no time to wonder—no way to change *anything*. The campaign tumbled to its close with a relentless ferocity that everyone tried to disown. No one could deny, though—the Dole campaign did "turn it loose."

Dave Owen found an account of Dole's war service in a vets' magazine; he had the story reprinted on hundreds of thousands of flyers, under the headline GUTS! . . . they dispatched crews in motor homes to hand them out—for days at a time, one Main Street after another. It was the first time the Bob Dole story had been told in anything other than whispers.

In the end, there was also a mailing to Legion vets, which alleged (in another headline): THE ONLY MILITARY TERM BILL ROY KNOWS IS AWOL. Then there was a little asterisk. You had to go to the next page to find a box that explained: Bill Roy was absent from the House of Representatives for two votes on military matters. (They'd happened to fall on Fridays—Roy was back in Kansas.)

In the end, there were stops at local high schools, where Dole would tell the kids, at the close: "Go home and ask your parents if they know how many abortions Bill Roy has performed."

In the end, the mudslinger ads went back on TV—no one seemed to think they were shocking anymore. . . . By that time, there were newspaper ads, too, showing a skull and crossbones: one bone was labeled "Abortion," the other "Euthanasia." Underneath, it said: "Vote Dole." By that time, the last week (especially that Sunday of the last weekend), there were thousands of flyers found on windshields. Those showed photographs of dead babies in garbage cans: "Vote Dole."

Dole said this stuff didn't come from him. He was trying to stop it. This kind of thing didn't help him!

But it did.

In the end, a switch of two votes per precinct would have made the difference. And one of the most Democratic precincts was around the Catholic church in Kansas City—Bill Roy lost there. His own Catholic precinct, in Topeka, he used to win two-to-one while running for Congress. He broke even in that one.

In the end, Bob Dole was returned to the Senate. On election night, his supporters gathered in jubilation at that Ramada, in Topeka. They could hardly *believe* it: they'd turned it around. They'd pulled it out! Dole could not believe it either. (He kept saying that night, "Well, 'fraid we didn't quite make it . . .") Dole would not come downstairs to speak till after two o'clock the next morning. Dave Owen said they had it won. The reporters downstairs said Dole had it won. The network TV said Dole had won. But Dole called 105 County Clerks before he would claim it.

Even then, there was no jubilation for Dole. Even while the crowd whooped and chanted his name, Dole had a stubborn grip on the facts. He was a winner, he'd escaped. He was going back to the Senate. But he wasn't going to go through this again. He could not. Something had to change.

———

How do you change a life that has lasted fifty years? With difficulty, and mostly at the margins. But Dole was lucky. There was a woman in Washington, Elizabeth Hanford, whom he'd called from the road almost every night of that bitter campaign . . . sometimes two in the morning—didn't matter—he always felt better when he heard her.

That election night, he was even later: he wouldn't call till he knew he'd won. He told her he wanted to celebrate with her, back in Washington. He was crestfallen when she said she wouldn't be there . . . she was scheduled to depart for three weeks in Japan.

Of course, that was one of the reasons he liked her: she'd

never be the type to sit home, waiting for him to finish his meetings. She never stayed home—unless she was sleeping, or working there. She was just as serious about work as he was. (Maybe more: she'd fret about next week's work, or next month's—as he never would.) She was a rising star in the capital, a member of the Federal Trade Commission. She was good-looking, soft-spoken, raised with the graces of the well-to-do in Salisbury, North Carolina (Lotta moneyy!) . . . she was smart, well schooled (after Duke, agh! *Harvard!*) . . . she demanded perfection from herself (they had that standard in common) . . . she was a woman who achieved, who *shined*, in his Washington world. . . . In fact, she seemed so polished, accomplished, he almost missed his chance.

He'd met her in '72, just months after his own divorce. Elizabeth was working as assistant to Virginia Knauer, the White House adviser on consumer affairs. Knauer wanted a consumer plank in the GOP platform, so she asked for a meeting with the chairman, Bob Dole. Elizabeth said, years later, that the minute Bob walked in, she thought: "My! What an attractive man!" Bob said years later, that after the meeting, he wrote her name on his blotter. But what happened at the time was . . . nothing.

In fact, he saw her again at the opening of Nixon's campaign headquarters in Washington . . . and at the convention in Miami . . . in fact, it was months before he called, and they talked pleasantly for forty minutes, about nothing in particular, a conversation that led to weeks of more . . . nothing.

After which, he called again, and they had another long talk—yes, they certainly did see eye-to-eye on many subjects! . . . But at the end of that call, all he could muster was that it might be nice to get together.

"Whah, yes!" said Elizabeth. She waited for him to name a place, a date . . . something.

But the poor man could not. There was thirteen years' difference in their ages: she was only thirty-seven—would she be interested? He was, after all, a man divorced, not a raging success in affairs of the heart . . . and she was the Belle of the Capital Ball!

So she was . . . but she was also, at that point, almost convinced that she had outpaced all suitors. There were men who thought she must be a tigress (and came on doubly strong to show their stripes); and plenty who thought she was great—if she'd only drop that government stuff; and men who never would get close enough to find out anything (it was the capital, after all, and she *outranked* them!)—to put it simply, she scared most men to death.

Bob was shy (he finally did choke out an invitation to dinner at the Watergate Terrace) . . . but not afraid. He was a man not unused to strong women (Elizabeth seemed a fragile flower next to Bina Dole). He was not worried about outranking her, out-politicking her, out-thinking, or out-talking her . . . those were stripes he'd proved elsewhere. His concerns were more innocent (and winning): mostly he wanted to prove he could be a nice date.

But he was! She was interested in what he *really* did . . . he didn't have to make small talk, make up hobbies, keep telling jokes. She understood his world, understood his talent in it. And still . . .

What he discovered, little by little (this was, perhaps, the hook that fetched him into the boat) . . . she was a woman of surprising innocence. There was her faith in the system: she believed government—public service—could make lives better.

There was her faith in the Lord, which she talked about with unaffected certainty that one did not often hear in Washington. There was her startling *un*certainty about herself, wherein, slowly, one discovered the fuel for both her compulsive work and her faith in a Higher Power. . . . When she got back from Japan, she found a gift of champagne and a dozen long-stemmed red roses. Bob Dole had a life to remake—he did not want to be alone.

That was almost the turn of the year—1975, the year they would marry. Bob never did propose. They just started talking about their future, together. In fact, Bob said he'd known for more than a year . . . before that election night. He said he was waiting, just to make sure he had a job.

Of course, once he had a job, he had work to do. So they waited some more, until the Senate was out, that December . . . which gave Elizabeth time to select a chapel (the Washington Cathedral) and to find a gorgeous white dress, a veil of lace, and the organist, and to ask the Senate Chaplain, Edward Elson, to preside. Elizabeth memorized and rehearsed her vows, Bob figured he could wing it. . . . It was a Saturday, nearly evening, and the small guest list, mostly family, heard Dr. Elson's welcome to the happy occasion, this solemn sanctification, this fulfillment of God's plan, and His command . . .

Dr. Elson paused, perhaps for breath. He hadn't yet turned to Bob and Elizabeth—much less, asked them anything. But Bob wasn't waiting anymore. His prairie voice echoed in the Bethlehem Chapel:

"I *dooo!*"

1975

By that time, Dole was making speeches about opening up the Republican Party, repairing what he called its "antipeople image." It wasn't enough, he said, to rail against welfare cheats. Everybody knew what the GOP was *against*. Republicans had to demonstrate they could also take care of the needy, that the Party was not against *helping people*.

What had got into Dole?

The shamans of the Washington tribe were confused: just when they had him neatly pigeonholed, the hatchet man went mooshy. (Was this some kinda trick? . . .)

Then he started in on *food stamps!*

Dole was a member of the Senate Select Committee on Nutrition (most members were Ag guys) . . . and he found out that people who needed food stamps had to *apply for eligibility*. They had to prove they were so poor, the government ought to sell them stamps worth, say, one hundred fifty dollars, for the princely discount of one hundred dollars. It took weeks, of course, to prove eligibility.

So in '75, Dole advanced an amendment: if people were hungry, sell them stamps *now*—let them *self-certify*. (If the paperwork didn't square, next month . . . well, time enough to deal with it then.) At the root of this proposal was a radical idea: *feed the hungry*—you could trust people, even though they were poor!

Well, conservatives sent up a howl. They were promoting a bill by Senator James Buckley to knock thousands (or tens of thousands) *off* food stamps . . . now Dole wanted to make the system work?

But Dole didn't stop there. With the Chairman of the Select Committee, he authored a complete overhaul of the program, a reform: for the first time, there would be an income limit for people who got food stamps (that was the bone for the conservatives) . . . but at the same time, the government would just give the stamps away. Dole was acquainting his fellow Republicans with another radical truth: people who were hungry might not *have* a hundred dollars for stamps.

Well, that sent up great clouds of ash from the op-ed volcano. It wasn't just Dole's radical ideas. It was his coauthor (to be precise, his coconspirator), the chairman of the committee, the Senator from South Dakota, and the right wing's favorite *piñata*, George McGovern. This reform was called the *Dole-McGovern bill.*

C'monnnn! . . . What was Dole try'na *pull?*

The wise-guy community was profoundly split on what everybody-who-knew was supposed to know:

Some knew for a fact that Dole was playing clever hardball to win a bigger market for the Kansas farmer. (It was true, Dole saw this as a spur to markets . . . but the Kansas wheat farmer didn't give a damn about food stamps.)

Some others descried a plan—*a plot*—to position Dole on issues of national substance, in furtherance of his overweening long-term ambition for higher office. (It was true, Dole meant to build a record of substance . . . but if he were picking issues out of a hat—why not postal rates?)

The Washington Post essayed the bold notion that Dole was actually trying to help people. A series of editorials commended Dole for his farsighted stand. (Of course, those truly in-the-know knew it had to be more than that—Dole was, you know . . . trying to Be Nice!)

Dole, himself, told anyone who asked: there was nothing miraculous here. Bill Roy almost beat him because voters didn't think he cared about *anyone* . . . wasn't true!

Well, how could the lunch-buddies accept that?

Everybody knew Bob Dole was . . . a hatchet man.

(They'd all heard what he said to Senator Buckley. They held hearings on Buckley's hard-line food-stamp bill. Dole asked—in open session!—"Agh, d'you put in a *burial allowance . . . f'the ones who starve?*")

But Dole kept making speeches, affirming that people who were hungry should *get food!* . . . In Washington, someone spotted him at a prayer breakfast. That was probably Elizabeth, got him to come . . .

Aha! . . . Elizabeth!

All at once, the official-secret story emerged. Elizabeth Hanford Dole (who was *so* nice!) was working on Bob.

All at once, everybody knew the *same story*—most satisfyingly well known—how Elizabeth sat Bob down (at home—yeah, in the kitchen, with the little lady!) . . . and made him watch tapes of himself . . . and showed him how to Be Nice! . . . She was *making* him *Nice!* . . . She was his *Nice coach!*

Well, Bob didn't go out of his way to correct that. Seemed to him, if there had to be credit, Elizabeth ought to get it. He probably *was* nicer, liked himself better—once he got past reelection . . . once the new Congress moved the capital past the Nixon bitterness . . . once he got to flyin' around the country . . . come home, there's Elizabeth—he *loved* coming home.

Matter of fact, he was in love . . . why wouldn't he be mellow?

For God's sake, he was getting good ink from *The Post!*

1976

When Dole got the call from Gerald Ford, at the GOP Convention in Kansas City, he was so excited, he blurted out: "Mr. President, I can't believe it!" Then, with his next breath, he accepted the Vice Presidential nomination.

A lot of people couldn't believe it. Elizabeth was stunned. The family went into a tizzy. Kenny told a reporter in the Muehlbach Hotel: "I'm looking for my cleanest dirty shirt." ABC had a crew on a chartered plane, already bound for Howard Baker's hometown—they had to U-turn in midair and head for Russell, Kansas. Nelson Rockefeller, the retiring Veep, had only hours to put together his speech of nomination.

"The man of whom I speak," Rockefeller said that night, in the Kemper Arena, "can take the heat! He can not only take it, believe me, he can really 'Dole' it out!"

With that rhetorical flourish, Ford's advance men appeared with blue-and-white Ford-Dole signs, still smelling of ink . . . but Dole's name set off a floor demonstration that lasted, alas, less than ten minutes. UPI was already on the phone to Bill Roy, who had the bad grace to bring up dead babies in garbage cans. "It may be," Roy predicted, "what some people will call a dirty campaign."

Newsweek called Ford's selection "impulsive," and called Dole the "cut-and-shoot junior Senator from Kansas."

The New York Times got hold of Phyllis (at that point, Mrs. Lon Buzick, wife of a cattleman and prominent Republican in Sylvan Grove, Kansas), who thought Bob would make a bored Vice President—too aggressive. But with Ford thirty-three points behind, Phyllis said, Bob might save the day. "Bob Dole," she said, "will just tear into Jimmy Carter. He is just as smart, and just as tough, and just as hard . . . he can campaign forever if he has to—even with the arm."

That's what Ford and Co. had in mind. The President would stay in the White House, conducting himself Presidentially. (Polls showed Ford lost support when he went out to campaign.) What Ford wanted was a running mate who would bleed Carter with a thousand cuts, make news, get the ink, take the heat . . . meanwhile, shore up the GOP in the heartland (where farmers still resented Ford's cutoff of grain sales to the Soviet Union).

Dick Cheney, Ford's Chief of Staff, told Dole: "You're in charge from the Mississippi west."

Bob Teeter, the President's pollster, told Dole they'd have to win (or win back) 130,000 votes each day.

Ford said: "You're going to be the tough guy."

It wasn't supposed to be a "nice" job . . . or easy. The point was, Dole had a chance! Point was, they gave him the ball! Bob was so pumped up, he was racing around his hotel, grabbing hands, spreading cheer. He had one phone to his ear and another uncradled, on the hotel bed—someone else waiting. He was *thanking* people. (Never did *that* before! . . .) He was so excited he invited Ford to begin the campaign in the *real* heart-land—Russell, Kansas—the next day! Tomorrow!

That was the first time Dole brought the national show to Russell, and it hit with such a jolt . . . the town would never be the same. *The President of the United States* was coming, twenty-some hours from now. The Air Force took over the nearest decent airport, seventy miles east, in Salina. The Secret Service choppered into Russell to pick out a site—the courthouse lawn. The Chief of Police called in reinforcements from a hundred miles; he placed them, with rifles, on the courthouse roof, the Legion roof, the buildings across the street; state cops poured in to help with traffic. Paramedics and ambulances arrived from nearby towns, the hospital went to alert: they had to have the President's blood type in stock. The telephone company strung hundreds of new lines. Ev Dumler, head of the Chamber of Commerce, borrowed three sections of bleachers, and trucks to carry them in; he tracked down a P.A., took all the chairs from the Armory, and from the 4-H, too; dismantled and hauled in the stage from the fairgrounds, along with stock tanks for icing down thousands of sodas (the President wanted an old-fashioned barbecue). Scores of Republican ladies brought their grills from home to cook twenty thousand hotdogs (a bakery in Hutchinson put on a special shift for buns). The VFW color guard was scrambled to attention, the high school band crashed into rehearsals of "Hail to the Chief," the Dream Theatre gave its marquee to the message WELCOME PRESIDENT FORD AND BOB, the radio station went live remote from the courthouse, the *Russell Daily News* swelled with extra pages of Dole-pictures, Dole-bio, Dole-record, and Dole-remembrance, all topped with the two-inch headline: BOMBSHELL HITS RUSSELL. . . . Of course, no one got any sleep.

Who wanted to sleep?

Mae Dumler, Ev's wife, said: "Well, I got so excited, I didn't know what to do. So, I just made a pie."

Bina Dole got so excited when the President was going to come *into her house* . . . she lost it, on her front step. She couldn't find her key. Fifteen men in suits were standing, waiting, while Bina scrabbled around in her purse, until Jerry Ford said, "Bina, let me have a look." Then Bina about dropped dead. *The President's hand* was *in her purse!* (Elizabeth, at last, found the spare key behind a drainpipe.)

That day, as Bob stood on stage to speak, the President, Bina, Elizabeth, and Robin sat behind him. The sun was shining on the people, massed so tight, they hid the courthouse lawn. There were ten thousand souls in Russell that day. At the edge of the crowd, at the curb, on Main Street, the farmers leaned against their pickups—Doran's friends. . . . Doran Dole had died the December before (Bob and Elizabeth cut short their honeymoon). Bob got the Vice Presidential nomination on August 19—that would have been his father's seventy-sixth birthday. What would Doran say if he could see his town, and his son, now?

"I am proof . . . ," Dole told the crowd, "that you can be from a small town, without a lot of material advantages . . . and still succeed . . . if I have succeeded.

"If I have had any success, it is because of the people here. . . . I can recall the time when I needed help . . . and the people of Russell helped . . ."

Then he stopped speaking. He looked down. His left hand came up to his forehead, hiding his eyes. He was crying.

The silence was awful. It went on for a minute—felt like

forever. Elizabeth wanted to go to him. No one knew what to do. Bob was sobbing, and could not stop.

Then President Ford rose from his chair behind Bob, and he started to applaud. And ten thousand people stood in front of him, clapping, cheering, until Bob looked up again and said, in a croak that was nearly whisper . . .

"That was a long time ago . . . and I thank you for it."

———

Jerry Ford flew straight from Russell to a week or two of golf in Vail, Colorado. Dole hit the road . . . and did not stop. He'd never seen a national campaign from the inside—now he was supposed to build one, on the fly.

Dole had Dave Owen doing money—Owen took an office in Washington (Eighteenth and L streets), slapped a couple of million Ford-for-President dollars into the Riggs Bank on the corner. That same day, Owen rented a Northwest Orient 727 for the next ten weeks . . . so there wasn't extra money to throw around.

In fact, it was a wicked combination—a plane, and not much money. For one thing, to pay costs, they had to rent half the plane to the press, who'd badger Dole constantly . . . and since they had the plane all the time, there was no point paying extra money to stay anywhere. So mostly, they'd fly Dole out and back—same day. To be precise, they'd load him up at National Airport for a godawful 6:00 A.M. hop to some breakfast, and do three or four stops across the country, picking up hours, heading west . . . by evening, they'd be in the Southwest or the Rockies, or on the West Coast . . . after which, they'd fly Dole back across the country all night. It did save money, and time. It just about killed Dole.

The demands were horrendous. Dole was supposed to hit every major media market . . . but concentrate on the farm states . . . but make news every day . . . and hit Carter, always, hit him, and hit him. Ford was in the Rose Garden. Dole had the press to himself. He did all the speaking. He needed things to say, and he had no issues staff, no speechwriters (save for his own humble Senate folk).

They were piling on staff as fast as they could: press advance and Larry Speakes from the White House; Lyn Nofziger, Charlie Black, and Paul Russo from the Reagan team. Dole tended to rely on his Kansans—Owen, Bill Taggart, Kim Wells . . . but he didn't listen to anyone, really, save to the White House, where Teeter's polls and Jim Baker's instincts determined the program (more farm stops, more and more . . .). On the plane, there was a continuous turf war, constant bickering about who was giving Dole the best advice. The last thing Dole would do was sort out that cockfight. True to form, Dole's staff did whatever it wanted—except for the ones he trusted, who did whatever he asked.

He was supposed to hit Carter . . . but hit him with what? So the Washington smart guys started a briefing book, which would travel on the plane, for the Senator's study. Within weeks, there were special briefing books, depending on the issue—all color-coded, so the *master* briefing book referred to appendices: "See Blue Book" . . . "See Red Book" . . . "See Green Book," and so on. It was weeks before Dole said: "Doesn't anyone on this plane know I'm color-blind?" So they stuck big labels on the books: "THIS IS THE RED BOOK" . . . "THIS IS THE GREEN BOOK." Dole never opened the damned things, anyway.

In fact, he was mild about Carter—by his standards. (*Time*

mag called him a disappointing "tabby cat.") Before his nomination, Dole said Carter looked like "southern-fried McGovern." But the White House Big Guys got nervous (southerners might be offended), so they warned Dole off that. Then Dole started telling his crowds: "I *used to* call him southern-fried McGovern . . . but I have a lot of respect for Senator McGovern . . ."

(That was true—and mutual: one of the first calls to Dole-for-Veep came from George McGovern, suggesting a few ways Bob might get under Jimmy Carter's skin.)

In his own view, Dole was "sticking to the issues." Carter was committed to the Humphrey-Hawkins bill for full employment. So Dole would suggest, at every stop, that a Carter White House would have two hotlines—one to the USSR, the other to the AFL-CIO. Carter could not make clear the arithmetic of his "tax reform." He had to clarify, then reclarify. Dole snapped: "Carter's got three positions on everything. That's why he wants three debates."

Actually, there would be four debates: for the first time, the nation would see the Vice Presidential nominees square off. (Dave Owen tried everything to scuttle that plan—to the point of making Ford's Big Guys watch a tape of Dole at the Kansas State Fair. But the Veep debate was scheduled, nevertheless.) Dole was supposed to take one day a week to study his briefing books and practice answers . . . but whoever made the plan for Dole to sit still in midcampaign could not have known the man. Elizabeth (who was on leave from the FTC) rode along with Bob for days, tried to engage him in pepper drills . . . but even with his new wife, Bob was not much for games. As the fateful date neared, Dole's thin staff devoted itself to preparation: they had to find a quiet, secluded space for practice (finally begged a room at Nelson Rockefeller's Washington estate) . . . they set up a studio to duplicate the stage Dole would find in Houston . . . they hired a video crew . . . they had Senators Domenici and Stevens help with new briefing books . . . they got Dave Gergen, one of Ford's top aides, to bring up questions and to play Mondale . . . it took weeks to get the thing set up perfectly, for practice. Then Dole wouldn't come. He sat in his office, making phone calls. Finally, on the last day, he came to the house, stood behind the podium, looked at himself on the monitor . . . and walked out.

It wasn't until he got to Houston, the day of the debate, that Dole would sit still to run through questions . . . but by then he was so offhand (or trying to look offhand), he'd just toss off wisecracks.

"I think tonight may be sort of a fun evening," Dole said, in his introduction to the national TV audience. He said he'd been friends with Walter Mondale, in the Senate, for years . . . "and we'll be friends when this election is over—and he'll still be in the Senate."

Dole seemed determined to keep this light. (Mondale, on the other hand, seemed just determined.) . . . But it's tough to be light with the nation's networks, a thousand of the nation's press, and tens of millions of the nation's voters judging every word.

How many thought it was funny when Dole said George Meany (head of the AFL-CIO) "was probably Senator Mondale's makeup man"?

How many thought it was funny—or fair comment—when Mondale linked Dole to Nixon and Watergate? . . . Or when Walter Mears, of the AP, asked Dole about his criticism of Gerald Ford, when Ford pardoned Nixon?

Dole didn't think it was fair, or funny. You could just about see his spine go stiff, his brow grow dark, as the anger took hold. He said he didn't think Watergate was an issue . . .

" . . . any more than the war in Vietnam would be . . . or World War II, or World War I, or the Korean War—*all Democrat wars* . . . all in this century."

Mondale's mouth fell open a notch, and hung there—he couldn't believe Dole had slipped into partisanship about . . . a world war!

But Dole didn't slip—he stalked in . . . and he didn't stop:

"I figured up, the other day: if we added up the killed and wounded in Democrat wars, in this century, it would be about 1.6 million Americans . . . enough to fill the city of Detroit!"

After that, Mondale let him have it:

"I think that Senator Dole has richly earned his reputation as a hatchet man tonight . . ."

Of course, Dole thought that was *so* unfair. He said, after the debate: "I thought I was very friendly. I called him 'Fritz' a couple of times. He called me 'hatchet man.'"

In fact, Dole was sure he'd won the debate—scored his points, made his jibes stick. It was a shock to him when the flood tide of editorial condemnation crested. ("Democrat wars" was common political discourse in Russell—like "Republican depressions.") . . . Dole tried to *explain*: he didn't really mean the Democrats *caused* all those deaths, those wars—he just wanted to let Mondale know, if he made Watergate a Republican millstone . . . well, there were weights to drag the Democrats down, too. He even hinted that if *anyone* had the right to talk about the suffering of war, it was *him*. Bob Dole! . . . You want to make something of that?

Of course, that only made it worse.

Why couldn't Dole just . . . back off?

All the hatchet-man Grape-Nuts that reporters had stored now came rattling into "analysis" pieces—character will out, after all! Pat Caddell, Carter's pollster, filled the breakfast bowls when he told the big-feet that Mondale was a plus for the Democratic ticket . . . but Dole was dragging the President down! This poop got to be so well known by those in-the-know, that Dole became the subject of the Carter campaign's only negative ad. (With four of the last six Vice Presidents moving up to the top job, who would *you* like to see a heart-beat away?)

Dole just kept flying. What else could he do?

In the last weeks, he hit four or five states a day—mostly through the Midwest and South . . . where he'd rasp out his message that the name of his candidate wasn't Nixon-Ford, it was Jerry Ford! . . . Carter could talk about trust, but Jerry Ford had earned it!

Dole was getting sick, his voice was almost gone. Elizabeth would call the Schedulers to tell them Bob *had* to rest—they were killing him. Then Bob would call and add a stop to the day after next . . . they were so close, just a little more push . . . they could make it—Carter could still go sour! . . . Carter's margins were melting away in Texas, Illinois, Ohio, Florida, Oklahoma—Dole got the tracking polls every day. Jerry Ford was, at last, loosed from the White House, and he thumped and stumped around the country, showing the grandeur of his office (thousands came out, just to see *Air Force One*) and the Every-man values to which he still clung (every Ford rally featured the Michigan fight song). There was a half-hour TV show in all the major markets, with Ford answering questions from that penetrating interviewer, Joe Garagiola . . . and lots of negative ads, feeding the public doubts about Carter.

And in the last week, the final Gallup Poll showed . . . Ford and Dole edging into the lead! . . . It wasn't really a lead—just one point—easily within the margin of error. But that statistical nuance was beside the point. They had come from *thirty-three points behind!* . . . On the last weekend, Ford called to say: "You're doing a great job. I know you must be exhausted—but keep it up. We're going to make it, Bob!" . . . They had climbed back to even—against all odds. And they were moving—Dole could feel it:

"I smell VICTORYYYY! . . ."

They lost by two percent . . . by fifty-seven electoral votes . . . by the barest handful of votes in Ohio and Hawaii. Those two states would have turned it around: if 9,244 votes had changed (one one-hundredth of one percent of the votes cast nationally, or one vote in every ten thousand), it would have thrown those two states to Ford and Dole . . . and completed the miracle comeback.

Dole had so many ways to measure how close they came— and how far they'd come: the farm vote held solid for Ford . . . Dole won all of his assigned states—the West, the heartland (save for Missouri—he was *sure* the Democrats stole that in the cities!) . . . Dole did not want to give up—they could demand recounts in the tightest states. . . . But Ford ruled that out, day after the vote.

By that time, Dole was in bed—fevered and weak. He only got up to host his party. He was giving a party for reporters who'd traveled with him. . . . That's when Barbara Walters asked the question—like a knife in his ribs:

Didn't Dole think, Ms. Walters asked, *he was the one who lost the White House for poor Jerry Ford?*

That sent Dole back to bed. How could she *say* that?

He did his job! . . . Did it well!

He showed he could play in the big leagues—the biggest!

He showed himself, anyway.

It was a couple of days later, when Dole got back to the office, Taggart asked: "Well, think you'll run for national office again?"

"Not for four years," Dole said.

Actually, he started just weeks after the vote—Dole did a speech in South Dakota, then a stop in Illinois, and then . . . he was flyin' around. He made sure to bring up the VP race himself.

"Well," he'd say, "they told me to go for the jugular—so I did . . . It was mine."

He knew he would run again—in four years, eight, or . . . as long as it took. Next time, he wouldn't do dirty work for anyone else. It would be his campaign . . . so he knew, it would start in Russell.

1988

When Bob came home a couple of nights before his announcement, November 9, brother Kenny Dole had to pick him up at the airport. Kenny and his second wife, Anita, went to Great Bend. They had to wait—two planes . . . Bob and Elizabeth flew separate planes. But it wasn't any more than two or three hours for Kenny—no more than usual. He didn't mind, though he groused about it the usual way. He always got the call when Bob needed fetching . . . a voice on the phone from Washington: "Senator says pick him up in Hays, nine o'clock tomorrow night." That was all. No questions. No please or thank you. If Kenny knew the voice, maybe he'd say something.

"Is he bringin' his sandals?"

"Uh, excuse me?"

"I thought Jesus Christ always wore sandals."

Kenny used to say he was going to start the BOB Club. "B-O-B stands for Brother of Bigshot." But he was used to it. He probably would have been offended if they hadn't called him, now that Bob was going to be President.

Kenny wouldn't say that, of course. In Russell, it's best not to talk about your dreams. But you could see the idea had got to him, like a flu making the rounds. Everybody had a touch of it, whether they'd admit it or not.

Russ Townsley, the newspaper chief, had been whipping up folks for months, trying to get all the businesses in town involved in Bob's announcement, not to mention the Chamber, the Legion, Kiwanis. . . . It got to be quite some pressure—like Russell had to pass this test for Bob, and for the country. The whole nation would be watching, Russ said. But as the big Monday drew close, it was easier, the fever took hold: the kids in the high school choir and band were practicing . . . their parents ordered signs for their storefronts, and bunting from Topeka . . . Bob's ex-wife, Phyllis, sent handsome handmade wooden buttons: DOLE '88 (Bob's Aunt Gladys Friesen sold them in Russell) . . . in Kenny and Anita's office on Main Street, you could buy tiny stone fence posts like the pioneers once carved in Kansas, except these said DOLE FOR PRESIDENT and sold for forty dollars a pair . . . Dean Banker got a sign for the front of his department store: BOB DOLE SUITED UP HERE FIRST . . . the men of the Russell Volunteer Fire Department polished the pumper they'd named *The Doran Dole* . . . the *Russell Record* printed every hopeful poll that came over the wire, and readied two special sections with pictures of Bob, his family, his house, his school, his campaigns . . . national reporters came to town in ones and twos, collecting "color," which could be anything down-home, folksy, or Kansan—anything at all about the town—so it got to be like everyone in Russell *had done something,* just by living there, and knowing Bob (though many were hazy on Bob; it *had* been almost thirty years). . . . It came clear to everyone that something big *was happening,* that it started with Russell, and people in the Chamber thought they ought to consider what would happen, you know, if it got to be like Plains, Georgia, or Abilene, with its museum for Ike . . . so it wasn't really politics—more like a *civic* thing, but emotional, because of the Bob Dole story . . . which was the centerpiece of this festival, like a passion play the town was putting on, about Bob (and the apostles, who were the family, the exiled Phyllis, and Bub Dawson from the drugstore).

That Saturday night, when Bob got home, Kenny made sure to drive him up Main Street, so Bob could see the banners (IT ALL BEGAN IN RUSSELL!), the new mural, the storefronts, the grandstands, platforms . . . then it was straight to Bina's old house. It was late, Bob and Elizabeth had to rest. Kenny would be back early the next day, to take Bob to the graveyard.

Sister Gloria had gone out to clean off Bina and Doran's headstones, and make sure there were fresh flowers. Doran had died in 1975, Bina eight years later. Gloria's own cancer was under control from chemotherapy, but she had only one kidney, and her blood pressure was just *shooting* up. The problem was the family reunion that Sunday before the announcement. Gloria had made a ham boat with twenty pounds of ham and pork—it was thirty pounds by the time she added twenty eggs and the rest of the trimmings. She'd made a loaf of cheese potatoes in the big electric roaster, and a load of candied sweet potatoes—from scratch, like Bina used to do. And two loaves of buttered French bread, a plate of pumpkin bread, a big black cherry salad, a cranberry-apple salad, fresh applesauce, a plate of cookies, a banana cream pie, and chocolate, cherry, and apple pies, a hundred-and-some cinnamon and pecan rolls, and homemade ice cream, with the cornstarch, like they always had.

Then Kenny called and said he'd invited that cousin from

the power company—he was a cousin, wasn't he? Anyway, the fellow said he'd be delighted, and now he was bringing sixty more "cousins" . . . so Kenny was yelling for help, and Gloria swung into a higher frenzy of cooking.

Gloria had a houseful, too, with her kids, their spouses and babies, all come back to town. And Aunt Gladys, Doran's sister, had all her beds filled . . . and *then* Bob asked her to take in Mrs. Kelikian. (She put her off on Faith and Harold Dumler, who weren't even family, but there was no choice—and Faith would do a lovely job.) Then Robin wasn't comfortable in Bina's house, where nothing had changed—nothing had been moved—since Bina died. There were all the fussy matching drapes, with valances, and the carpets, and Doran's favorite chair. But there was no more scent of honeysuckle, rose, wax, or baking bread . . . no life. Robin thought it was creepy, like sleeping in a shrine. So she came to Gloria's and asked if she could stay. Gloria didn't have a spare inch, but she took Robin in, put her with her own girls.

After the graveyard, Bob and Elizabeth went to the Methodist Church, where three rows in front were roped off for them. Aunt Gladys was hoping for a word with Bob, after the service, but his back was turned—he was being interviewed. After that, it was Dawson Drug, which was packed with press and photographers, and then to the 4-H for the family reunion. There were more than two hundred people there, and it almost broke Gloria's heart. Bob was working the whole time. He didn't get to eat anything. They had red-checkered table-cloths . . . and they were paper. There were six Republican women in the kitchen . . . they didn't know what to do with the food. The fourth cousins ate like they wouldn't get another meal all year. Bob was busy shaking hands. He took more than an hour, working his way through the crowd, and then he was gone. Kenny had to take him to the hospital and the nursing home.

Elizabeth came over to Gloria's. She was hungry again. Gloria fixed her some chicken noodle butterball. When Elizabeth finished, she said, "That shore was good!" And Gloria said, "Cherry pie?"

"Whah, yes!" (Gloria never could figure why that woman didn't weigh three hundred pounds.)

That was when Gloria got to ask how Bob was—she asked Elizabeth . . . who said Bob was just *saying,* the other day, how pleased he was to be coming home to Russell. Elizabeth was sure the welcome had touched Bob's heart.

Gloria was going to doll up and go to Bob's party at the VFW that night—they were going to show Bob's new video. But when the time came, Gloria didn't feel well . . . Aunt Gladys got everybody in her house together—she had ten in tow—got them out to the VFW. But by nine, when she arrived, she couldn't get in the door.

People were backed up from the door of the hall. It was dark inside. Everyone was watching the video. It was spectacular— all about Bob's childhood, and Russell, Bina and Doran . . . Bob went off to war, and came back, just broken bones and heart . . . he picked himself up, and never forgot . . . and by the end of the film, when he's running for President, standing in a cornfield, making a speech, with the cornstalks eight feet tall around him, and that wonderful music welling up under his words—when he talked of opportunity, freedom, our future . . . you were guaranteed to end up crying if you knew Bob, or his folks, or the town— or even if you didn't, you felt like you did. Even the reporters stopped talking (there were hundreds staying over that night—some had to sleep in Hays). The people from Washington—staff and smart guys—you could almost see it dawn on them: this stuff they'd been *saying,* Dole and the heartland, small-town, hardworking . . . it was *real,* here it *was,* the Veterans of Foreign Wars, Post Number 6240, Russell, Kansas . . . they were *in it!* And as the lights came up, everybody was talking at once—wasn't that *great?* Did you see that picture of Bob, so *skinny?* . . . And people who knew him, even slightly, felt they were *part of something,* something great *was happening*—no one left the hall . . . except Bob and Elizabeth (who had to go, so Kenny took them) and Gladys—she got in the back door, saw all those strangers, and just went home.

———————

"Good morning, ladies and gentlemen," said Dave Owen—first at the microphone on Main Street, early that Monday. "Good morning, and welcome to Russell, Kansas!" There was a cheer from the big crowd, shivering in shadow. The sun still hadn't peeked over Banker's Mercantile, to the left of the stage. The wind was blowing straight down Main Street, the temperature was in the twenties, the air was frozen clear.

Up on stage, behind Dave Owen, stood Chuckie Grassley from Iowa, Bill Brock, Bob Ellsworth, and every Republican official from Kansas. To the right of the stage stood the Russell High School Bronco Pops Choir, which warmed up with its choral rendition of "Twist and Shout." Then the emcee, Russ Townsley, got the mike and boomed out:

"Boy! On a morning like this, does *anybody* doubt they're in Kansas?"

Behind Russ, Doran Dole's old grain elevator was the first building to catch the sun. From the top of the tanks, a banner announced: RUSSELL, KANSAS. HOME OF BOB DOLE. Townsley was in a transport of local pride. "I say, *'Hey, America!'*" he yelled. *"'You take a good look at who we are!'"*

Russ introduced Larry Ehrlich, Chairman of the Russell County GOP, who said: "We *know* he's going to make it . . ." Then Bob's old friend and opponent, the gentlemanly former Governor, Bill Avery, stepped up to talk about three icons of Kansas Republicanism: Huck Boyd, Alf Landon, and Dwight Eisenhower. The Russell High School Bronco Marching Band followed up with a fight song, and the kids in the bleachers were waving little flags, as the sunshine, at last, lit them in sharp glare. Cheerleaders cued them:

"Go Bob go!

"Go Bob go!

"Eatem up! Eatem up!

"Go Bob go!"

When the band swung into "Yankee Doodle Dandy," the Bobster emerged from Dawson Drug, stage right, and climbed onto the platform. He was wearing a gray topcoat and red power tie, and was bouncing to the music like Bob Crosby of the Bob-cats. Elizabeth was splendid in purple. Robin matched entirely, in rose.

Russ Townsley read out the telegram received in Russell, in May of 1945. "The Secretary of War wants me to express our deep regret . . ." Then, Bub Dawson was on stage: "If I can take you back forty-two years . . ." Bub talked about the collection for Bob. "There was a cigar box on the counter," Bub said, "with Bob Dole's name on it."

Then . . . *Bub produced the cigar box*—the relic of the passion play!

But this time, the box contained *one hundred and thirty-five thousand dollars* . . . from Russell, Kansas . . . for Bob's campaign.

The band played "God Bless America," an up-tempo rendition—fast, in fact—it was still cold as hell. Nancy Kassebaum, Dole's Senate colleague from Kansas (and daughter of the icon Alf Landon), had the honor of introducing Bob. "In a real sense . . . ," she noted (no flies on Nancy!), " . . . Russell is what this campaign is about."

And when she said the name, kids screamed, "Dole! Dole! Dole! Eeeeeeeeeeeeee!" and the band let loose with "Step to the Rear (and Let a Winner Lead the Way)" . . . and there was the Bobster, in front now, with a smile of fierce elation, bouncing to the music, swinging his arm—bringing on the action!

Lord, what a story! An American Everyman drama for our age! And not done yet—no! Bob had a speech to make . . . but first, his part in the drama:

There was a woman who'd traveled with him to Russell, Sophie Vavlety, a strange Park Avenue New Yorker who was in love with Bob Dole, and everything he touched. She gave her fur coat to the Mayor's wife at the airport. She gave Kenny a lambswool Italian scarf, and Anita a silk kimono. She gave two dresses to Doris Henderson, the owner of Russell's Country Squire Motel. Sophie was an emblem of Bob Dole's new world, which he'd brought back to Russell. Now Bob called the Mayor to the stage and presented, from Sophie Vavlety:

A $10,000 check for the poor of Russell, Kansas.

Well . . .

Bob still had to speak . . . but what was left to say?

What were *words* about the opportunity, compared to this allegory-in-life of righteous GOP redemption? . . . What were prosy visions for the nation's next four years, compared to the miraculous *fact* of Dole's life—his *future*—sun-sharp and solid as the bricks on Main Street?